The Simple Joys o[f Kayak Fishing]
(Angling Tips and Tales from an Old Guy in a Plastic Boat)

Dedicated to:

The Old Guys Who Like to Fish (OGWLF) – Scott Taylor, Harry Steiner, John Veil, Terry Hill, John Rentch, Keith McCray, and Bruce Kellman. Our outings together have produced many fish and even more laughs. Thanks to each of you for sharing your time with me and showing me the way.

Special appreciation is due to Terry Hill and John Veil.

Terry introduced me to kayak fishing. A longtime coworker and friend, he intrigued me with his stories of striper catches from a kayak in the Chesapeake Bay. Once he had my interest sufficiently piqued he took me shopping and helped me find the perfect boat. He then took me on my maiden kayak fishing trip. We have since spent countless hours together on the water. Even though he and his wife have recently moved to the Carolinas, I look forward to more hours on the water with him in the near future. Surely, stories of Terry kayak fishing in coastal Carolina are waiting to be made and told. I want to see them first-hand.

John Veil inspired me to write this offering when he published his excellent book, Fishing in the Comfort Zone. He has been my technical advisor and editor for this, my first publishing effort. Most of all, he has been a great fishing companion. He has generously shared locations, advice and knowhow with me. He has made me a better kayak fisherman. I would not have contemplated writing this book nor could I have completed it without his encouragement and assistance.

Preface

This is my kayak fishing story. This is also a fishing book with relatively few fish pictures. That was deliberate on my part. This book is about the joy that kayak fishing brings to me -- the new lease on my angling (and retired) life that my plastic boat has provided. It's an attempt to acknowledge and thank the fine people who have helped me discover kayak fishing. While not precisely focused on catching fish, I offer sound advice on where, when and how to put them in your boat. More so, it presents my personal observations of angling from a seat near the water. It's about being close to nature in the Chesapeake Bay and other waters. It's about the camaraderie of like-minded people. It's about the elation I feel on every kayak outing whether I catch fish or not. It's a bit opinionated in that I challenge some kayak angling trends here in the Chesapeake region. But it's mainly about the simple joys of kayak fishing. I offer this short story with the hope that after reading it you will both understand my passion for the hobby and find the same feelings of exhilaration in your own kayak.

My kayak – The new lease on my fishing life.

2

Chapter 1
The beginning

Fishing has been a prime pursuit for me almost for as long as I can remember. From the time my parents let me roam freely from my backyard at six or seven years of age (a far safer time then) I often traveled a lengthy path through the woods that surrounded my neighborhood to Marley Creek. There while sitting on the bank I would catch shiners, which at the time I thought were white perch, and my most coveted prey, bullheads. For years I used only a stick, line, bobber and a hook.

The stick was a sapling of an unknown tree species that I found growing in the woods. I would cut a new pole each spring, 5 to 6 feet long. It had to be straight with a nice taper to provide a little flex in the tip. I would shave all the bark from it. Imagine that – a kid in elementary school with a knife. Then I would toss the stick on my father's garage roof to "cure" in the sun for a few days. I doubt my father knew that I could climb onto the roof by scaling a rabbit hutch behind the garage and hopping from the hutch to the garage roof. I also knew how to climb the walls of my elementary school (after hours of course) to get the playground balls kicked to the roof by my classmates during recess. But that's a story for another day.

The line I used was actually Dacron braided fishing line, probably 30 or 40 pound test that I purchased at the only department store I could reach on my bike without crossing the forbidden barrier of Ritchie Highway. Yes, braided line was quite common 55 years ago as was a small section of fishing tackle in the upscale Hutzler's Department Store. You don't see this even in J.C. Penney or Sears today. The braid then wasn't as tough as the braid we have now but it existed. I would also buy a small round white tin can of assorted hooks. I preferred the long shanked Aberdeen hooks in the tin. I liked them because they were easier to remove from the fish. My outfit was complete with a plastic red and white bobber.

My bait was either earthworms or dough balls pinched from a fresh slice of bread. Because my trips to the creek were often early morning pursuits, the bread served the dual role of bait for the fish and brunch for me. The likelihood of the bread becoming my snack was inversely proportional to the bite of the fish. I never succumbed to that fish/snack ratio when I dug worms for bait!

When I wasn't fishing I was reading about fishing. I loved the old "Fishing in Maryland" magazine with its glorious maps, pictures of huge stripers and articles by Bill Burton. The maps had little fish symbols peppered throughout. How nice I thought. If I could only get on the water, I'd know precisely where the fish were! There were also other symbols and notations on the maps that provided endless fascination for the mind of little boy. Things like "wreck" and the really mysterious, "dumping grounds." Just what was dumped there? I had no idea but my primary school mind could imagine all kinds of things to entertain the intellect of a second grader.

In time I graduated to a real fishing rod. I saved my meager allowance and finally the day came when I had $25 stashed in a jar that my mother kept for me in the kitchen. My father drove me to "2 Guys" department store in Glen Burnie and I bought a Mitchell 300 spinning reel and a Garcia fiberglass rod. I suspect my father covered any budget shortfalls to complete the purchase. I still have that reel and rod. And since that purchase, I shudder to think how much money I have spent on fishing -- baitcasting and spinning rods, fly rods, miles and miles of lines, dozens of tackle bags and boxes, thousands of hooks, bucktails, feathers, jig molds, tying vises, angling books, and of course a lot of fishing trips in my ever expanding pursuit of the hobby.

I will spare you the details of my 50 plus years of angling. I will concentrate instead on the most recent. It has been during that time that perhaps the most versatile angling aid imaginable entered my fishing arsenal. I purchased a kayak. It was an unlikely pairing. Here I was, an old retired guy, squeezing into the contoured confines of a chunk of plastic and propelling it by expending my own energies. Shouldn't this be the time in my life when I buy a sleek center console and power my way around the Chesapeake with the aid of dead dinosaurs feeding a Honda four-stroke? That works for some. But what I'd like to share on the following pages is the joy that kayak fishing brings to me.

Some of what follows may be instructional but that's not my main goal. There are plenty of books telling you how. I'd like to tell you why. I suspect if you already fish from a kayak you may find a validation of your pastime in these pages. That's OK. A little affirmation is good for everyone. But if you're on the fence as to whether a little sliver of a boat can take you to new fishing heights, I hope these pages encourage you to find out for yourself.

My first rod and reel. An antique like me. But we both still work!

Chapter 2
My fishing progression

By far, even at my present stage of my life I have caught more fish while standing on a bank or wading in the water than I have while floating. Despite growing up in Anne Arundel County, Maryland surrounded by water, no one in my immediate or extended family owned a boat. No one owned waterfront property either. In fact, no one in my family fished. I often wonder how I got the fishing bug. Clearly it wasn't genetic. Nevertheless, it struck and I have "paid" for it with time and money since. Time and money well spent, I might add.

So I became a committed bank fisherman. That was rather difficult given the paucity of public access to the Chesapeake Bay or non-tidal water for much of my life. That access has improved greatly in recent years but for those of us now in our 50s and 60s who grew up in Anne Arundel County, public water access was sparse during our youth.

The biggest change for my fishing fortunes was simply maturity. With it came higher education, a real job, decent money and perhaps most important, wheels. Once I achieved each of those life milestones my fishing horizons expanded.

I met others where I worked who liked to fish. They exposed me to lures. Prior to then I was a bait fisherman. I was in my mid-20s and I had never caught a fish on an artificial lure. My work friends gave me a good natured teasing and accused me of "monkey fishing". The connotation of that term was that bait fishing was so easy a monkey could do it. I have subsequently learned that drifting bait over a hard bottom for croakers takes great skill. But the monkey fishing moniker steered me first to my Mepps spinner period and ultimately to my fly fishing period.

The very first fish I caught on a lure was a white perch on a Mepps Aglia spinner from a tidal pond on the Patapsco. From that point forward it was game-on for me and artificial lures.

Then it so happened that a co-worker introduced me to fly fishing. After I caught a bluegill with a fly rod popper in a Crofton Pond the long stick became my preferred method of angling.

Fly fishing requires lots of room for the back cast. When fishing from a bank you have to be careful to not hook trees or an unsuspecting passerby with your back cast. So I naturally became a wader. Fishing while standing in the water away from the bank gave me the space to cast and a new freedom to move and wander. And wander I did. I walked many miles in the upper Potomac River, the upper Susquehanna, the Shenandoah, the Juniata, the Yellow Breeches, the Cacapon, and closer to home the Patapsco at Avalon. Fly fishing instilled me with a desire to move relentlessly while fishing. No longer did I tolerate fishing a small area from a bank nor did I like to be anchored in a boat. My eyes were constantly looking ahead to the next riffle, the next rock, the next grass bank, or the next downed log. There was always a fish waiting for me (I thought) at the very next spot. Goodness only knows how many fish I left in my wake by my travels. But I certainly enjoyed the journey, catching trout, sunfish, catfish, suckers and countless smallmouth bass with my fly rod.

Despite the exhilarating and liberating feelings that wade fishing brought to me there was a significant problem. The rivers I waded were far away from Anne Arundel County where I lived. The closest required an hour to reach. The farthest was more than 100 miles away. Aside from the gas costs, time was the most critical expense.

In order to stay closer to home and long before I had a kayak I purchased a new Old Town Canoe, a Discovery 174. It was a beast of a boat at 17 feet long and 83 pounds. At that time, I lived in a community with water access near the Bodkin Creek and Patapsco River. I made a cart out of old bicycle wheels so that I could walk the Old Town canoe to those destinations directly from house. My two children and my wife often joined me on canoe paddles in the Bodkin Creek and I could fish from it solo if I turned it around and sat in the front seat to keep the bow down. Otherwise wind would grab the canoe and take it places I certainly I didn't want to go.   That canoe gave me a degree of the freedom I was seeking on local waters. But I also learned that its weight was an inhibitor to its use. It was difficult to transport by car and to be honest it sat far too long between outings. I eventually traded it to a neighbor for an intricately detailed wooden goldfinch that he carved. It was a good deal for both of us at the time.

The first plastic boat in my fleet.

My next foray into boating was a used aluminum 12-foot Sea Nymph V-Hull with a trailer and a Minn Kota trolling motor. It was too small for the Bay proper. I would take it "locally" to Piney Run, St. Mary's Lake or to Pennsylvania parks with lakes such as Codorus and Gifford Pinchot. But again, it sat too long between uses primarily because of the lack of suitable access to the water near my house. I couldn't justify the cost of the keeping the trailer tagged and the boat registered. Plus, it took up an entire side of my garage.   I sold it to yet another neighbor who subsequently took it to his vacation cabin on a West Virginia lake.

As my career and family obligations grew, my time for fishing dwindled. But my desire to be on the water and for that freedom of movement while fishing remained. I was in fishing limbo. I wanted desperately to wade rivers but life's demands and time got in the way. Time flew by. Soon I was nearing sixty, facing retirement and to make matters worse, I had a painful health issue to deal with. I didn't think I was ever going to clear the dust off of my fishing tackle.

Gathering dust.

Chapter 3
Kayak to the rescue

Two years into retirement from a lengthy career in the Department of Defense and starting a second lease on a pain-free life thanks to a wonderfully skilled neuro/brain surgeon at Johns Hopkins Hospital, I was ready to pull on my waders again. No doubt my old Hodgman's would need patching and my felt soled wading shoes had been outlawed in Maryland since I had last worn them. State authorities correctly addressed the possibility that felt soled shoes could transport invasive species of plants and organisms leading to algae blooms and whirling disease. I would miss the rock gripping ability of felt soles but I bought new shoes with rubber soles and I was set to hit the pavement traversing I-70 and I-83 once more to fish my beloved rivers. But something got in the way – a small plastic boat.

My friend and former co-worker, Terry Hill, told me he was catching stripers in the Chesapeake Bay from his kayak. I was shocked. My initial thought was that kayaks do not belong in the Bay. They're too small and likely to get swamped by waves or run over by power boats. Second I had no idea where you could launch them. My experience growing up was that water access was for the well-to-do with waterfront property or at marinas with boat ramps where you had to be a paying member. Third, I wondered if I could I fly fish from a kayak. Actually on this last matter, I knew I could cast while sitting down. During my fishing progression I had learned to do that quite well from a canoe and my little V-Hull. But to fly fish for tidal species was another matter. My fly fishing had been mostly fresh water. I was filled with questions about the prospect of kayak fishing.

Before long, I was in Terry's truck on guided a tour of outdoor stores and kayak distributors in Annapolis. I was like Goldilocks tasting the possibilities. In my porridge that day I learned about Sit-On-Top kayaks and Sit Inside kayaks. I learned that some were too heavy for me to carry. Some were too short to carry me. Some were too long and too unwieldy to lift. I learned about tracking and stability and then I saw the most magnificent thing in a kayak – pedals. I became a convert without even trying one. I purchased a Hobie Revolution 13. I was a kayak fisherman. There was only one problem. I didn't have clue how to use the boat. That led to another problem. I didn't know where or how to catch fish from it.

Terry took me on my maiden voyage in Whitehall Bay launching from Mill Creek. It was May and there was still a slight chill in the early evening air. The water to my touch felt warmer than the air. It was a beautiful spring late afternoon. I left my fly rods home and brought spinning rods to my ease my transition to kayak fishing. This was primarily going to be a get acquainted mission with my Hobie. I literally had never been in one before. Such was my trust in the brand and my acceptance of Terry's positive stories of the many anglers who used them in the Bay, I hadn't test-driven my boat before purchase.

The pedaling motion came as natural to me as walking. Soon I was slicing through Mill Creek heading toward Whitehall Bay. I was absolutely enthralled with my freedom of movement. I was so excited I lost Terry! I couldn't see him at all. I could see ships in the far distance queued up for entry in the Port of Baltimore. I could see the Bay Bridge from a vantage point I had never viewed it from before. But I had absolutely no clue how to get back to our launch site. The entire shoreline looked the same to me. I knew I came out of a creek but I doubted if I could find it on my own. I momentarily thought my first voyage might be my last. But if it was I wanted at least to catch a fish. And I did. My first kayak fish, like my first fish on an artificial lure was an obliging white perch caught near the rocks at Hackett Point on a jig with a curly tailed grub. Mind you, I was such a novice about Bay locations I didn't even know that point of land had a formal name.

Soon after my white perch victory, I caught a glimpse far off of paddles moving up and down. It was Terry. He had been out on a trolling jaunt. I was relieved and I decided to stay put so he could join or (in truth), rescue

11

me from my wayward journey. We pulled our kayaks to a nearby beach and rested a bit before heading back. I was completely captivated by the scenery -- the Bay Bridge rising before me even closer than before, the gentle waves slapping the rocks around Hackett Point, the birdlife flying overhead and landing in the water near us.

On our way back to Mill Creek, Terry shared a productive fishing site with me. He took me to a nearby oyster bar where he had previously caught stripers. He said, "They're over there about 100 yards out from shore," pointing directly to a distinctive landmark on the bank. "Over there" I went and I cast a Rat-L-Trap exactly where he showed me. Bam! I was hooked up. This fish pulled harder than any smallmouth I had caught in the rivers. It was an 18-inch striper, a healthy fat one. I was impressed with its energy as I reeled it in and with its beauty as I pulled it onto the deck of my kayak. The fish was a mass of muscle in constant rhythmic motion as it broke itself free from my lure and flopped about my pedals. I finally subdued it and returned it to the water.

Striped bass are extremely attractive fish. The dark lines on their sides are the perfect accents to their overall shape and conformation. Although I'm not a meat fisherman, releasing almost everything I catch, I instantly understood the stripers' magnetic hold on the Bay's anglers. Even if they weren't extremely tasty, their looks alone would warrant them their title as Maryland's state fish.

Additionally, Terry's precision in locating the striper I caught impressed me. He knew exactly where they were holding and graciously shared the location with me. I thought to myself, "He also must have read 'Fishing in Maryland' with those little fish markers on the maps." From that evening on I have been hooked on kayak fishing.

The site of my first kayak fish with Bay Bridge in the background.

Terry must have read the "Fishing in Maryland" maps!

Chapter 4
My new view from the water

That first trip was harbinger of good things. Terry and I fished many outings that first year. I grew comfortable in my Hobie Revolution (Revo for short) and I learned my way around some of the tidal waters of Anne Arundel County. In the process of doing so I realized the similarities of kayaking angling and wading a river.

In both you have the complete freedom to explore your chosen waters. In fact, in a kayak your freedom is expanded because you can negotiate deeper water and you can go farther and travel quicker than you can on foot. A kayak therefore gives you a greater chance to catch fish. A simple fact is this. The best fisherman in the world cannot catch fish when fish are not present. A kayak is great tool to help you find the fish.

Wading and kayaking are both exceedingly relaxing pursuits that allow you to feel as though you are a part of the environment. Kayaking may grant you even closer access to your surroundings than you'll ever obtain by wading. While in a kayak you're more likely to become a curiosity to river otters, terrapins and blue herons than you would on foot.   You're low to the water and less of a physical threat to wildlife in a kayak. Plus, you are spewing no exhaust or noise from your kayak via a sputtering carbon-laced motor to alert or startle nearby wildlife. I've gotten very close to a variety of aquatic, terrestrial and avian lifeforms in my kayak and each has provided a pleasant visual accompaniment to my fishing.

On a recent kayak fishing trip to Tampa, Florida I was thrilled to have dolphins swim directly under my kayak. Actually, I was probably more thrilled after they left the scene. During the actual event, seeing those big grey fins and rounded backs swimming directly toward my bow gave me pause. I waited anxiously for the split second it took the dolphins to swim under my kayak fully expecting one of them to rise under my hull and dump me into the water. But that didn't happen, thank goodness.

Later that same morning, I was again startled, this time by a loud snorting sound directly behind me, literally within a few feet of my stern. I turned and saw the snout of a manatee and two big dark eyes still underwater staring at me. I would like to provide a picture but of the many photos I took, you see nothing but two nostrils barely poking above the water. With an average weight of 1,500 pounds, manatees have to keep most of their body in the buoyancy of the water. The creature slowly submerged, suspended in the water column and floated away. But it didn't go far and was later joined by another manatee. For hours they stayed in my immediate vicinity.

Closer to home, I am intrigued by the wildlife on the Chesapeake Bay. I recall an outing in my Revo in a tidal pond of the Severn River fishing for pickerels. I wasn't having a good day. I had had no hookups, just few taps and a couple of tentative follows. In short it was a common pickerel outing for me. If I can digress here, I'll never understand how those toothy fish can be so tentative. Stripers never play around. They hit lures with gusto. White perch slash at artificial baits. Largemouth and smallmouth bass are so determined they rarely miss top water plugs. But a pickerel can drive you crazy with feigned interest. Anyway, I was floating in this pond and an osprey crashed down 50 feet in front of me and flew off with a pickerel. After that word must have gotten out on the osprey hotline because several more arrived and made successful aerial attacks. In their hunting frenzy, they were not deterred at all by my presence. I enjoyed the show.

But other times they clearly do not want me near them. Ospreys often nest on channel markers in the Bay or on platforms provided for them. I thoroughly enjoy the view my kayak gives me of their life cycle throughout the spring and summer. The larger of the two, the female, stays on the nest to incubate while the smaller male brings her food. Before long, the male brings food to her and their chicks. I've watched individual osprey nests from spring to late summer. It's a gratifying experience to see the offspring sitting on edge of their enormous nest testing their wings for flight. However, if you get anywhere close to a channel marker or platform with an active osprey nest and linger, you'll hear first from the female as she screeches her displeasure. If the male is circling above nearby, he'll join the chorus and let you know you need to depart the premises. I've never had one swoop down on me but I've never loitered to found out if they will.

My understanding is that our Chesapeake osprey pairs are monogamous for life but they separate after their chick rearing duties are done. Then they migrate apart, not as a pair, flying as far away as South America where they spend the winter. Yet they will return in the spring, reunite and use the same nest that they used the year before. Their navigational ability is beyond amazing, as is their fish catching skill which I've often witnessed.

She's not happy with my presence nor is her mate overhead.

Another (friendlier) close encounter I remember was with a river otter in a creek of the Severn River. It swam directly beside my Revo for maybe 10 yards as I pedaled my way upstream. I really believe it was interested in observing me up close. It showed no fear. Later it joined another otter, its mate I presume, and they performed an aquatic ballet in front of my Revo rolling repeatedly in the water like two playful puppies.

Unexpected observations of nature can happen in your kayak. Sometimes creatures you don't expect to see on the water suddenly appear. On one of those occasions I was startled by a deer leaping from the bank into Mill Creek. I presume it was going to swim across the creek but it appeared to be as startled by me as I was by it. After going maybe 50 yards with only its head above the water it turned around and swam back to the bank where it leaped onto shore over a wooden wall and disappeared into the brush.

A deer in the water!

Another surprise finding happened to me in the middle of Whitehall Bay. I was heading to Hackett Point. I was several hundred yards from shore in 12 to 15 feet of water when I noticed what looked like a coconut bobbing in the water about 20 yards off my port side. I felt compelled to investigate so I altered my course slightly. I soon noticed the coconut had

17

a head and four legs. It was a box turtle swimming across Whitehall Bay. I was completely astounded and watched it intently. It was not going in circles but was headed on a steady northwest course.   It was a good half a mile from shore in the direction it was heading so I decided to help it on its journey. I scooped it up and took it in the same direction it was going even though it would have been closer to take it to my intended destination, Hackett Point.   I beached my kayak near the mouth of Mill Creek and took the turtle into the woods and let it go. I presume (hope) that a new generation of box turtles owes its existence to the ride of that particular turtle in my Hobie.

Out for a swim in Whitehall Bay...

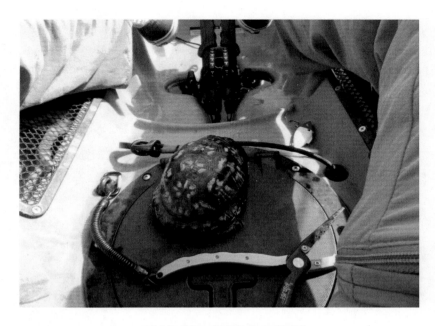

...and hitching a ride in a Hobie.

And finally, some of my observations of nature while seated in my kayak illustrate the harshness of life in the wild and how quickly it can end. I was casting a Clouser Minnow parallel to the riprap wall at Horseshoe Point on the Severn River, a great place for white perch on a summer day. Above me I heard a terrifying screech and then a thumping sound almost like a fastball hitting a catcher's mitt. I looked up just in time to see the aftermath of a raptor that had smashed into a pigeon a mere 30 feet above me. That pigeon had chosen a very inopportune time to cross the Severn. The hawk continued its missile-like flight over the point with the pigeon locked in its talons. Left behind were feathers of various shapes and sizes fluttering down upon me and my kayak like snow.

What all this means is that catching fish often becomes an afterthought on my outings. It's nice to catch fish of course. That's my main purpose in going out. But I can be completely mesmerized by the everyday observations of various lifeforms in the wild. Add to that the initial breezes of warmth in the spring, or a gentle summer rain, or the changing colors of the leaves and the first coolness of the air in the fall and I am so very thankful I can be on the water in my small quiet plastic boat to experience these splendors. I believe a kayak is the ideal mode of travel to put you close to fish and all the wonder that the surrounding natural world offers. That's why I enjoy kayak fishing.

Blue herons are a common sight in Chesapeake waters.

Chapter 5
Fishing alone in group

Finding a good fishing buddy is almost as important as finding a good spouse. Compatibility is essential. It helps to agree on certain angling tactics or at least to be flexible enough to tolerate the fishing preferences of others before joining them on a trip. It helps to be pleasant and encouraging with your fishing companions. There is no room for jealousy, disingenuousness or pettiness of any kind. Perhaps most important, you must be willing to share information on techniques and locations, being generous with the former and discrete with the latter when you receive the same in turn.

Most of us are privileged to have a group of particularly good friends that we like to fish with. I certainly am. Those of you fortunate enough to read John Veil's excellent instructional book, <u>Fishing in the Comfort Zone</u> have already been introduced to my circle of kayaking angling companions. I am part of the Old Guys Who Like to Fish, OGWLF for short. As John describes in his book most of us are retired from our careers and take every opportunity we can to join each other on the waters of the mid Chesapeake in our kayaks. Weekdays are preferred for our outings for the obvious reasons and hardly a week goes by in season when we do not have at least one trip joined by all or a few of the members of our group. There are no membership fees, no designated officers, no written by-laws in the OGWLF and we gladly welcome newcomers. The knowledge and encouragement I have received from these gentlemen have been enormous. I have grown in the hobby exponentially thanks to them and most certainly, I would not have had the confidence to write this book without the information they have so generously shared with me.

I enjoy our outings so much that sometimes on the night before an OGWLF outing I have difficulty sleeping just like I did on Christmas Eve when I was a kid. The prospect of fishing new or even familiar waters with my friends is that exciting to me. That said one of the things about kayak fishing I like is the freedom it gives me to be part of a group and yet I can still make independent decisions on the water.

I rarely venture out alone in my kayak. Being with others gives me a sense of security and also camaraderie. However, many of the tidal areas I fish give me choices. Do I want to troll or do I want to cast? Do I want to work natural shorelines or do I want to cast near and under docks and piers? Do I want to look for schools of predators churning up a patch of water or do I want to fly fish in a creek or a tidal pond?

The beauty of kayak fishing is that you can rig appropriately to be flexible so that you can change tactics during trips. I do that often. I can carry up to five rods in my Revo and I may bring fly rods in addition to conventional rods on outings. While my friends are trolling I may be off on the shoreline casting to structure.

Of the fishing techniques I employ, trolling is my least favorite. However, it is also perhaps the most effective for putting a lot of stripers in the boat at given times of the year. I am often in the fray with other OGWLF members doing long loops in a productive area picking off fish after fish. It's exciting and it's hard to leave an area when fish are present in such large numbers. Everyone is gleeful at the constant hookups. There is laughter and shouts of exuberance coming from every kayak in our small armada as we paddle and pedal through stripers completely engrossed with our bucktails, soft plastics and crankbaits. But sometimes I like to hunt for the fish. While I'm trolling my recollections of wading rivers come to mind. I see a point of land, a riffle behind a breakwater or a seam in the water where two current flows meet. I know those areas should hold fish. It's hard for me to stay on my trolling course (even if I'm catching) when I see such promising areas. Therefore, I may break from the pack and try my luck casting.

I recall one spring day when the OGWLF were onto schooling stripers in the Severn. Stripers were prevalent and large. It was one of those days when the fish were begging to be caught. But I succumbed to that incessant call in my head to pursue fish on my terms. I broke from the pack and headed to a nearby tidal pond. No one else was present. There I worked my 7 weight fly rod and was perfectly content to catch pickerels.

While I was doing that I had my hand-held marine radio on and I knew my buddies were in the middle of an epic day of striper catching. I could hear their calls on channel 68, sometimes receiving just fragments of their calls because my line-of-sight to them was obstructed. But I heard things like, "25 inches on that one; I've got two on at once; damn this is fun; that's number 15, etc...." I knew they were catching a lot stripers and I was genuinely happy for them. But I was also genuinely happy for me. I had the tidal pond all to myself and the pickerels were very agreeable to my Clouser Minnow offerings. I didn't catch as many fish as my friends caught nor were my pickerels particularly large as far as pickerels go, but I fished the way I wanted. I was fishing alone in group. A kayak is the perfect tool for that kind of fishing.

We start together but rarely stay that way on the water.

Chapter 6
Radio waves

"Colonel Bon'jay, Colonel Bon'jay.   This is the power yacht Raptor calling. Come on."

A little interpretation is order. This transmission is a frequent reception in my kayak on my marine radio. It is from my good friend Terry. For some reason, even though I was never in the military he commissioned me as a colonel. He also took my surname which is of German origin and turned into French.   I have spelled his moniker for me phonetically as he pronounces it on his calls.   His identification as "the power yacht Raptor" refers to Terry's conversion to a Hobie Outback from his original kayak which was a Santa Cruz Raptor, a paddle-powered boat. Lastly, Terry's handle on Snaggedline.com, a wonderful internet chat forum for Chesapeake kayak anglers is "Raptor".

What did that call mean to me? It meant fish were nearby. Terry and I had progressed greatly in our kayak fishing exploits since that day I caught my first kayak fish with him Whitehall Bay.   I had pedaled my Hobie for two years and 600 miles since then. Plus, I now had electronics in my repertoire – a fish finder and a hand-held marine radio. But by far my best fish finder was Terry himself. Just like our initial trip together, we had separated on this particular excursion and we could not see each other. He was at Greenbury Point on the Severn and I was not far from the mouth of Mill Creek, a long haul by kayak. But Terry's call meant he was into fish. Off I went, moving my Revo fairly quickly while pacing myself for sustained pedaling on a long ride.

The interesting thing about Terry is that he has no electronics on his kayak other than his radio. Yet he knows from experience where fish are and he has cataloged in his memory the depths and contours of key places where we fish. Sometimes I'll look at my fish finder and ask him how deep he thinks the water is and he'll invariably tell me the right answer within a foot or two. He'll also confirm to me where ridges and depressions in the bottom are.

When I reached Terry at Greenbury he was trolling just inside the mouth of the Severn. I came upon the bow of his yellow Outback and as he got close to me, his feet busily churning his pedals, he lifted a 20-inch striper from the water with his right hand and said, "The fish are so thick here all you have to do is reach down and grab one!" That's typical Terry humor. He saw me closing in and held his last catch below the waterline to surprise me. But kidding aside, he has an uncanny ability to find fish. Terry and I traveled over 15 miles that day between Whitehall Bay, Mill Creek and the Severn. I lost count of the stripers we caught. Most were schoolies but a few met the 20-inch keeper limit. I would not have caught half of them without his call.

When John Rentch, another OGWLF member, went on his first outing with our group he mentioned at the launch site as we were packing up to leave that he didn't have a particularly good trip. He said he just couldn't find schools of fish. I told him, "That's easy. Next time follow the guy in the in yellow boat."

This brings me to the primary point of this chapter. A hand-held marine radio is an incredibly important tool to enhance your kayak fishing experience. It provides a valuable safety feature that allows you to easily make an emergency call on channel 16 should you need to. Some radios have GPS capabilities and can send your location to rescuers. You can also dial into National Oceanic and Atmospheric Administration (NOAA) weather forecasts. In fact, in some models forecasts will break into your regular channel with emergency weather alerts. Mine did that one afternoon and the call almost caused me to have the big one – cardiac arrest. Fortunately, it was a test of NOAA's emergency weather system. I was 40 minutes from the launch site when I heard that call. I was quite relieved when I realized it was a test, not a real weather emergency.

All these safety features are well and good. In fact, you can stress those features to your spouse to justify your purchase of a marine radio. They can be pricey depending on their features so a budget proposal to the boss may indeed be necessary to purchase one. Safety usually tips the scale in buy/no buy decisions.

But marine radios also have an excellent practical utility aside from safety and for those uses a basic inexpensive model will suffice. They allow you to stay in touch with your kayak angling companions while you are on the water with them. Typically, discussions between kayak anglers are short and often cryptic, especially when fish are biting. The reason for that of course is that others, not in your group, or worse yet, power boat anglers who can quickly infringe on your spot may be listening! Precise locational data is avoided but other more generic information is freely shared. Data points such as the depth where the fish are, color and style of effective lures, and tidal movement and current direction are often topics of discussion. Getting specific time sensitive information on any of those items can put you onto fish.

A marine radio can also entertain, especially if you are off on your own out of speaking range with your buddies. Sometimes the only chatter you'll hear on channel 68 is mundane. You'll hear working crabbers complaining about their empty pots. If you're near Annapolis, you'll hear water taxis and tour boats giving passenger counts. You'll hear infrequent but illuminating calls from charter captains comparing catch data. But you may actually hear interesting discussions. I once heard two sailboat captains talking about their voyage up the east coast from southern ports. In fact, their discussion was so long that someone chimed in and told them to take it to a cell phone. That person who admonished the sailors was correct by the way. Channel 68 is not for lengthy discussions.

Only once have I participated in a non-fishing discussion on channel 68. I was casting poppers near the wooden wall at Hackett Point and I heard two boaters having a casual conversation. One asked the other, "What's the name of President Kennedy's yacht?" With no answer forthcoming after a long pause I said, "Honey Fitz" into my radio. One of the boaters said, "What's that?" I repeated my answer. He said, "No, no. It was the Manitou." Feeling chastised, I kept quiet. Later that evening, I looked for the answer on the internet. It turns out we were both correct. The president had a sailing yacht named the Manitou (built in 1937 in Maryland) but he also renamed the motorized yacht used by prior presidents after his grandfather. He called it the Honey Fitz.

I learned it's best to stay out of other people's conversations. However, I continue to listen. My radio has become a very important addition to my kayaking equipment for safety, fishing information and entertainment.

Don't leave the launch without it.

Chapter 7
The other stuff I carry

All my kayak angler friends have various accessories screwed, tied or glued to their boats. I am no exception. It's part of the fun of kayak fishing to customize your boat for your fishing style. But one of the biggest mistakes I see from people new to the hobby is that they rig their kayaks before they fish with them. In some cases, they have "tricked out" their kayaks beyond any reasonable expectation of utility. Plus, they have made them heavier and more difficult to transport on land or certainly they'll take a lot of valuable time "loading them up" at the water's edge. If you think I'm kidding, watch kayak anglers at a launch site. Many take longer to get their boats in the water than a power boater at the Sandy Point ramp with a 24-foot Parker.

I have avoided the temptation to accessorize for the sake of doing so. I had my Revo for two years before I drilled a hole in it. That was to mount a fish finder, which I find more useful in marking distance, depth and underwater terrain than in actually spotting fish. Of course two of those data points, depth and terrain, are important in finding fish habitat. The device does its intended job for me.

Because a kayak is such a small boat, you definitely need on-board storage that will both secure your rods and tackle and make them handy to reach. Commercial rod holders, or homemade ones from PVC pipe are basic necessities in most kayaks. I've carried up to five rods but most of the time I bring only two or three. I also use a crate behind my seat for storage.

But as I have evolved in the hobby I find that I am leaving more things home that I used to carry. I no longer leash my rods. I used to keep them tied to their holders when not in use, although I always unhooked them while they were in my hand. I found the leashes cumbersome. I have never had a rod pop out of its holder either from a hooked fish while trolling or by choppy water and I have never dropped one. However, I do use rod floats just in case the aforementioned happens. The foam floats do not interfere in the slightest with the line on my fly rods or my conventional rods, including low profile bait casters. I view them as inexpensive and unobtrusive rod security.

Most of my kayak angler friends view a lost rod or two annually as a cost of doing business. I agree with them on basic principal. It's not the end of the world and all things considered, quality rods and reels are replaceable at moderate cost. But I have a sentimental attachment to my rods. Some of them are 25 to 30 years old and some are custom made. They have served me well and I would not be pleased if they were to "sleep with the fishes" forever more.

My array of conventional rods includes ultra-light, light and medium-light spinning rods and medium weight bait casting rods. Each of these rods is a freshwater rod (and each works well in the Bay) and each has a purpose and something it does better than the others. The trick is bringing the right rods for what I encounter on the water on a given day.

Most of my trips are species specific. If I'm trolling for stripers, I'll bring my medium light spinning rods or medium weight bait casting rods. If it's summer I might also bring a light spinning rod for casting small lures to perch at various stops on my way back to the launch. It's good to be prepared for a change of plans.

I can also use the same rods I troll with to cast lures to structure. Often these are the exact lures I troll – paddletails or twister tails on 1/2–ounce jigs, bucktails, and crankbaits. Years ago I learned that largemouth and smallmouth bass hug shorelines and structure at certain times of the year and at certain times of the day, lowlight conditions mostly. Fortunately, striped bass are no different. I was ecstatic when I learned this because it meant my preferred fishing style, honed by many hours on distant freshwaters would work well in local tidal waters while I was seated in my kayak. I firmly believe that the annual migration to the Bay Bridge by many kayakers seeking legal-sized stripers overlooks the fact that the stripers also like shallow water, especially in the fall and spring. Kayakers and power boater in particular pass many decent fish on their way to the pilings that support the Governor William Preston Lane Jr. Memorial Bridge in their search for a striper to remember.

If I'm going after pickerels or white perch, I'll bring two light spinning rods to augment my fly rods. One spinning rod will have a 1/8-ounce jig spinner on it and the other will have a small crank bait or a jig with a soft plastic trailer. This setup also works for various ponds on the Eastern Shore when I target bass and crappie.

Many kayakers carry knives and some have them adorning their PFDs. Knives are a necessity for those who fish with bait. But I've seen knives on kayakers that call to mind the famous Crocodile Dundee line, "That's a knife." They're huge. One reason given for the knife is to use it in emergencies to cut yourself free of rod leashes should you flip your kayak. That certainly makes sense in theory but in the panic of actual practice, I suspect it may be a difficult task. Since I don't use rod leashes anymore, I've dispensed with carrying my Swiss Army Knife. The only cutting tools I carry are stainless steel line clippers for changing lures and braided line cutters on my fishing pliers. I don't disparage those who carry knives. From experience I just don't feel that I need one hanging from my PFD.

Another thing I've cut down on greatly is the amount of tackle I carry. I am big fan of the Plano water proof tackle boxes. I have my lures and flies organized by type in individual Plano 3640 boxes. I also keep a few spare boxes at home so that I can create a single box to carry what I need on a particular trip if I am going to target multiple species. I rarely carry more than two Plano boxes with me on a trip.

There are three reasons that I can get away with so few tackle boxes on the water:

First, my trips rarely last more than four hours. If I used every fly or lure I carried in my two boxes I could not do so in four hours of fishing. Second, on each of the rods I carry I tie a different lure or fly. I'm more apt to change rods than lures. Frankly, on many trips I never open a tackle box.

The lures and flies I've pre-tied on my rods almost always suffice for my fishing. Lastly, I don't use a wide array of lures. I catch most of my fish on jig heads, a few proven crankbaits, spinners, streamers and poppers. They will hook any fish worth catching that swims in fresh water ponds or Chesapeake tributaries.

My one concession to accessory extravagance has been a BlackPak. Many call it a $125 milk crate and they are not far from wrong. But I like its sturdy construction, and most of all I like how I can configure it as a rod holder for both conventional rods and fly rods. My Revo is space challenged. It's also a fast and light-weight kayak, two very important attributes to me. I counter its sleek design and lack of deck space with a relatively expensive (I admit) storage alternative. Another thing I like about a BlackPak is that I can pre-load it the night before a trip so that I am ready to go at first light. Lastly, it's a good place to carry water, snacks and even spare parts and tools to do emergency maintenance on my Mirage Drive.

On this latter point I recall my first trip in my Revo to Wye Mills Lake. I was pedaling along quickly as I normally do when I fly fish to cover as much water as possible. I was laying poppers into downed wood while simultaneously moving my kayak forward when I came to a grinding sudden halt. I had hit a submerged stump with my fins. I didn't see it in the tannin stained water. One of the fins partially ripped from the stainless steel shaft. I removed the Mirage Drive, pulled my tool box from my BlackPak and slipped off the damaged fin and then realigned it back onto the shaft. It worked for the remainder of the trip, but I replaced both fins afterward.

Anchors are an interesting accessory. Some kayak anglers profess to need them and others do not. I've never used an anchor on my Revo. The pedals allow me to hold position in most currents or I can easily circle around to reclaim my casting positon. Also, I tend to move a lot while fishing, not to the same degree as trolling of course, but I frequently use wind and current to drive me along a promising shoreline.

My first experience with kayak anchors was with guide Neil Taylor of Strike Three Kayak Fishing in Tampa. The mode of fishing there is using paddle kayaks and casting in open waters largely unprotected from wind. An anchor is imperative in those conditions to hold position and avoid drifting out of range or worse yet, floating over feeding fish. In addition to the anchor I was introduced to the trolley system, an ingenious device for precision positioning of your kayak. Pulling the trolley forward or aft will allow the wind to spin your kayak in the desired direction for casting. Further, the "clip on" mechanism of attaching the anchor line to the trolley allows you to free yourself of the anchor should an emergency require you to do so.

My Native Ultimate 12 came with two anchor trolleys installed. I dutifully purchased an anchor and line for it but I rarely use it in the Chesapeake's creeks and tidal ponds nor do I use it often in fresh water. It's just not my style to fish a long time in any one location. I like to move about. However, an anchor is a good thing to have on seriously windy days.

The last item I'll discuss is a first-aid kit. It doesn't have to be a fancy store bought box. I made my own by tossing a few Band-Aids, alcohol pads and gauze in a plastic lunch bag. I keep the bag conveniently located in my Revo's center hatch so that I can reach it quickly. Cuts and scrapes are inevitable to anglers. But my fear, especially with all the fishing I do in warm tidal waters is Vibriosis. This is an infection caused by the Vibrio bacteria which can occur in warm Chesapeake waters. It can enter the body through open cuts and wounds. I've further read that people over 60 years of age can be particularly susceptible to the serious infection that the bacteria can cause. Since I have reached that magical age of increased risk, I immediately douse any cuts or scrapes I get on the water with an alcohol pad and then I cover the wound with a Band-Aid. I've been fairly fortunate thus far. But once due to an untimely wave as I was holding a Clouser Minnow between my thumb and forefinger, the hook on the fly buried past the barb into my thumb. A quick yank, and a painful wince, removed the hook but my blood was flowing freely from the tissue torn by the barb. I grabbed my first-aid kid and cleaned and patched the wound as fast as I could.

In summary, I'm glad I was equipped to handle my Mirage Drive breakdown on Wye Mills, the misplaced hook in my thumb, and having contingency gear such as an anchor can be a useful at times. But my point remains that I believe some kayakers make too many modifications to their boats and carry far too much equipment and tackle. I do realize that my fishing preferences dictate my conservative approach. Kayaker anglers now regularly take on big water offshore, something I would never do. Locally many kayak anglers visit the Bay Bridge for stripers, although I would dispute from ample experience that they do not need to go there to catch legal stripers. Clearly, kayak anglers who routinely compete for space in areas dominated by motor boats or those who fish in the ocean need more safety and contingency equipment than I carry.

On the other hand, I believe my kayak has made me a better fisherman because I have learned to use what I have onboard. Space is naturally limited by the small dimensions of a kayak and I have to be selective in what I carry. Much of the tackle I use is multipurpose and that helps me greatly. But I also make a conscious effort to limit what I carry to what I know will work for the situations I encounter.

Finally, I believe a basic joy of kayak fishing is being in quiet waters inaccessible to most boats. I don't want to compete with boats in crowded fishing areas. If I did I would buy a boat. I'd rather be in four feet of water casting to a shoreline in than bobbing in heavy seas. My advice therefore to pending kayak anglers is to think hard about how you expect to fish, especially before you invest in a kayak. A boat may actually be a better and less expensive choice for those of you who need a lot of "stuff" to go fishing or for those of you who think you need to be in big water to catch legal-sized fish.

My set up for a typical outing using the BlackPak as a rod holder.

Inside the BlackPak – Lures, water, snacks and tool box.

Chapter 8
Kayak fly fishing

I love to catch fish on the fly. It reduces fishing to its most basic form in that you manipulate the line with your hand both during the cast and the retrieve. There are no gear ratios to help you speed up the retrieve or to crank in a big fish. When a fish is hooked you can feel the power of the catch directly in your fingertips. You rely on your grip on the line and on the flex of the rod to subdue a fleeing fish. The drag, if needed at all, is often applied with the palm of your hand directly on the spinning fly reel. Fly fishing is therefore a very tactile way to fish. That's why I enjoy it so much.

Yet I realize many anglers are intimidated by it. They think fly fishing is too hard or too specialized. They think it's only for catching rainbow trout in streams or rivers. Certainly popular literature and the entertainment industry would lead you to believe that. Many books have been written about the near mystical experience of lofting a dry fly toward a wary brown trout. The writings of John Gierach and Norman Maclean illustrate the artistry of fly fishing. Actor Brad Pitt immortalized Norman Maclean's novel in the movie "A River Runs Through It," a must-see film for all fly fishermen. Pitt's main character in the movie scoffed at the idea of using live bait or anything but a dry fly to catch trout.

Undeniably trout are fun to catch on the fly. River wading is a wonderful experience as I've discussed in this book already. But the Chesapeake Bay and its tributaries, indeed tidal waters in general, offer many opportunities for fly fishing. Add a kayak to the formula and you have a very effective fish catching combination.

"Don't you have to stand up to fly cast?" That's a question I hear most often when I tell folks I fly fish from my kayak.   The answer is no. With good casting technique and a properly balanced combination of line to rod you can get more than enough distance to effectively fly cast while seated.

That brings me to the issue of standing in a kayak. I'm amazed at how many prospective and current kayak anglers want to know if they can stand in a particular kayak model. Indeed, many kayaks are advertised as being stable enough to stand in while fishing. I believe standing is a vastly overrated capability for a kayak and unnecessary in most kayak fishing situations.

I absolutely never stand while fishing in my kayak. (In addition to my Revo which does not encourage standing my Native Ultimate 12 paddle kayak is advertised as a kayak you can stand in.) In my opinion standing in a kayak is analogous to that old football adage about the forward pass -- Three things can happen and two of them are bad. When standing in a kayak you may catch a fish. That's good. But you can also fall overboard. That's bad. And you can spook the fish. Again that's bad.

This latter point about spooking fish should not be taken lightly. A kayak gives you the advantage of stealth in most close fishing situations. When I am pickerel or bass fishing, I may be floating within five feet of a shoreline and casting parallel to it. While seated I am low to the water and not easily seen by fish in shallows 40 to 50 feet in front of my boat. Even though our waters are often turbid, fish can still see us approaching -- especially if we create a six or seven-foot silhouette in the sky by standing. If I were to stand, I would immediately reveal my presence to the very areas I am targeting with my casts. Why would I want to announce to wary pickerel and bass that I am here to catch them? That's what standing does. Instead of standing to make a longer cast it is much better to stay low and patiently float to within your casting range. The kayak gives you the luxury of doing that. You are foregoing a very basic advantage of kayak fishing if you do otherwise.

To emphasize this point, a good fishing friend told me about a trip he took in a small boat with another angler to areas he normally visits with his kayak. They targeted pickerel and they did not do well. He attributed some of the pickerels' reluctance to bite to the larger footprint of the boat and the fact that the anglers in it were standing.

I will admit that it is harder to make long fly rod casts while sitting. However, here's another revelation: You don't have to make long casts to catch fish in your kayak. Your kayak can quietly put you into advantageous sites that negate the need for long casts. I rarely cast more than 50 feet from my kayak. One of the beauties of a kayak is its stealth. It allows me to get closer to structure and the fish than in a conventional boat. I simply don't need to cast far to catch most fish in the Chesapeake.

I have also noticed by making shorter casts that hook-ups are easier. The nature of fly fishing is that your hand is holding the line when the fish strikes. Wind and waves are inevitably going to put slack in your fly line. It's not like trolling or continuously retrieving a lure with conventional tackle where the line is taught. In those cases, the fish hooks itself most of the time. In fly fishing you hook the fish after the strike by raising the rod tip and simultaneously pulling the line with your hand. Those two motions remove the slack and hook the fish. The less line you have out the less the slack and the more hook-ups you'll have. It's that simple.

While long fly casts may be good for impressing your kayak fishing buddies, they'll do little to help you catch fish in the Chesapeake. Save them for when you're standing in a river or chasing bonefish in Florida. Shorter casts in your kayak in the Chesapeake and in other tidal waters work just fine.

Another advantage of shorter casts is line management. The less line you throw the less slack line you have to deal with. Space is limited in a kayak. There is no room in either of my two boats to carry a stripping basket and certainly no room to drop slack line on the deck. I keep my pliers and jaw spreaders (essential for pickerel fishing) on my deck between my legs handy for use. If I were to drop my line inside my kayak I would soon have a tangled mess and I would inadvertently toss my tools overboard.

I solve this problem by dropping my line directly into the water on the left side of my boat with my stripping hand. This is similar to wade fishing where you simply allow the line to fall to the water. The only difference is that your kayak may be drifting in the current and you may float over your line if you are drifting left. That's generally not a problem with floating line. You merely pull it from under your boat before sending out the next cast. But it can be annoying when using sinking lines. In that case it pays to position your boat so that you do not float over your line. That may reduce your targets or take you a little longer to get into the proper positon to reach them. It's not an insurmountable problem for sure but something to be aware of.

As proof of the efficacy of kayak fly fishing I can point to the fact that I have won the fly fishing division of the Chesapeake Bay Kayak Anglers (CBKA) tournament held every September for three consecutive years from 2013 to 2015. Now humility requires me to reveal that my winning catches were not particularly large fish nor were they numerous. In fact, that is typically the case when I fly fish at any time. I can usually catch more or larger fish with conventional tackle. But that's not my goal when I fly fish. I like the aesthetics of fly fishing – the bend of the rod, the unfurling of the line and tension of a hooked fish as I hold the line in my hand.

I've had particularly good success with a fly rod while kayak fishing in Tampa, Florida. Once I caught eight different species in one morning. Even my guide was impressed and featured me that day on his Facebook page. My catches on the fly in Florida have included Jack Crevalles, gafftopsail catfish, pinfish, sheepshead, speckled trout, gag grouper, ladyfish and needlefish. And I must say my favorite fish to catch on the fly in Florida is a ladyfish, also known as the poor man's tarpon. They are fast strong swimmers and they go airborne when hooked.

On one visit to Tampa, I hooked into a ladyfish at least 2 feet long. It put up an excellent fight severely bending my 8 weight St. Croix rod while making several long runs and jumping repeatedly. The fight was made even more exciting by high winds and waves. The Native Ultimate I was using was shipping water as I fought the fish and I knew we would have to head to shore soon. I also had two spectators very interested in my ladyfish. Two cormorants watched the fray and when I finally got the fish into the kayak they swam to my port side and sat bobbing in the waves within arm's length of my gunnels. When I released the tired fish, both birds dived after it but popped up soon thereafter with empty beaks. At that point I had to get out of the high winds and back to the safety of the beach.

Locally I've had wonderful summer days picking off white perch from Eastern Shore sod banks with a five weight rod. It's continuous action and sometimes I'll carry a fly rod just to end my day of chasing stripers with conventional tackle by casting flies to willing white perch. One evening I tempted fate (and the DNR police because I have no lights on my kayak) by staying on the water close to sundown in Kent Narrows. Schoolie stripers were swirling in the fast current and they found my foam fly rod poppers irresistible. I lost count of the fish I caught and released that evening. Another memorable catch for me was a 19-inch striper that hit a foam fly rod popper within a foot of the wooden wall at Hackett Point. I radioed to my friends that it sounded like a cinder block hitting the water when that fish sucked down my popper. Lastly, pickerels are great fun to pursue on a fly rod. I use the same flies for them that I do for stripers – Clouser Minnows and foam poppers. Pickerels may hit a streamer very subtly. You may not feel a strike but you'll feel a weight on the end of your line. However, when they hit a popper there is nothing subtle about it. Savage is the word that comes to my mind.

If nothing else, I hope my encouraging words about the ease of fly casting from a kayak and a few stories of my fly rod catches will inspire you to give the long rod a try. If you do I doubt you will give it up. I believe it is actually a simpler fishing process than using conventional tackle. You can carry less gear than most fishermen and still catch the main targets of interest in the Chesapeake and its tributaries. Plus, I think there is no more enjoyable sensation in fishing than actually holding the fly line in your hand with a fish on the other end. It's far different than "reeling one in." Please give it a try and see for yourself. And then I urge you to join me in fishing next September in the CBKA tournament with a fly rod.

For those who want to know more about the technical aspects of fly fishing from a kayak I direct you to an article I wrote for the CBKA website.

Fly fishing in Tampa.

**You can indeed fly cast and catch plenty of fish while seated.
Photos courtesy of John Veil**

Clouser Minnows, crystal buggers and foam poppers are the primary flies I use in tidal waters.

One of my foam poppers for freshwater. Bass love them.

41

Chapter 9
Tying one on

I began tying flies shortly after I started fly fishing in the 1980s. My first creation was a wooly bugger, a great all-around fly that I still tie and use successfully today. To be honest I never progressed much beyond the basic flies – Clouser Minnows, crystal buggers, and foam poppers for bass and elk hair caddis and nymph patterns for trout. One reason I never got excessively creative in my tying is because what few patterns I tied worked well. I felt no desire to mess with success.

My theory about fishing is that it is better to fish a few flies (and lures) well rather than fishing a large variety of different lures and flies looking for that miracle bait. My fly fishing mentor, the best fly rod bass fisherman I ever met, did not tie his own offerings. The only fly he used was a green Gaines Bass King popper in size 4. He ordered them directly from the Gaines factory by the gross. He bought so many that that Gaines thought he was a retailer. He was a magician with that fly. He cast it with pinpoint accuracy to structure. He would sidearm his casts to skip the popper under overhanging branches. I even saw him curve the line to drop that fly behind obstructions. And he manipulated the popper with just the right action – subtle twitches or hard snaps depending on the mood of the bass. I recall a day we stood side by side in the Susquehanna casting for smallmouth bass. We both had the same Bass King popper on our lines. Our splash downs were within feet of each other. Yet, he was out-catching me two to one. Clearly it was the action he was imparting to his popper that made the difference. I'm convinced his success was due to his familiarity with that fly, his confidence in it and his intuition of working it the way the bass wanted it. As much I admired my mentor's discipline to use only one fly, I could never copy him. I like using different lures and flies but I still probably carry fewer variations than most anglers.

My kayak friends unknowingly got me to expand my outlook in this matter. They were having great success trolling bucktails. It occurred to me that a bucktail is nothing more than a big Clouser Minnow. Or more precisely, given how long bucktails have been in use, a Clouser Minnow is a small bucktail. I had never tied one before but I decided if I could make Clousers I could tie bucktails. I bought a Do-It mold, poured my own lead jigs, thanks to donations of old sinkers from my friends. I powder painted the jigs and tied bucktails on them. It took me a while to learn how to get the hair evenly distributed around the jig but once I mastered that I began supplying my friends and myself with bucktails. Two of my ½ ounce ties are below:

Before long I was also rehabbing bucktails. My friends would give me a well-worn bucktail, even some I hadn't tied and ask me to send it to the paint shop and hair salon. I really enjoy reviving an old bucktail. Most have a lot of fish left in them if given a little attention. Those that are too far worn -- usually that means the hooks are broken -- can be re-melted to form new jigs. But most jigs can be revived before they get to that point. The following two photos show how a jig can be rejuvenated:

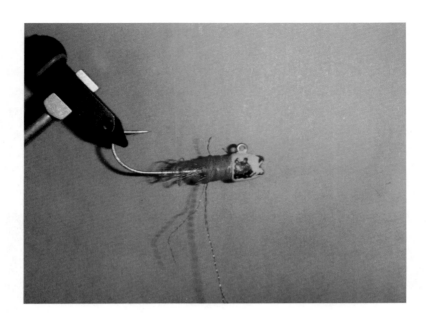

Before

After

After a spring striper blitz when attention turned to white perch, I noticed that my kayak friends were having great success with 1/8-ounce jig spinner combinations. Some spinners they had bought in stores and

44

others were locally made. So I designed spinners in my own style. I poured smaller jig heads and I found on-line suppliers for the necessary hardware (blades, wire arms and split rings) to build my own. These have proven effective for perch, pickerel and even stripers:

On a late fall day, a number of OGWLF group members were spread out in two Severn creeks. Our primary target was pickerels since the perch had long before left the shallows. I was working a shoreline with my spinners and I kept catching stripers – decent ones on light tackle, 16 to 20 inches. They were tight to shore in areas normally reserved for pickerels. I radioed to my buddies that these "darned stripers" kept intercepting my spinners. They informed me they were having the same striper "problem" and in fact some of them had begun successfully trolling for stripers in the creeks.

I've tried artificial materials for the tails on my ties but I keep coming back to bucktails. I believe natural materials pulsate better in the water than artificial material and are less likely to foul (wrap around) the hook. I'm not sure color matters except to the angler. I make them in shades pleasing to my eye. I've yet to have a specific color combination rejected by the fish. But if I follow any regimen with them, I use dark colors on overcast days and bright colors on sunny days.

Once again my kayak has expanded my enjoyment of fishing. If my fellow kayak anglers had not had success trolling bucktails I never would have thought to tie my own. And had they not showed me success with jig spinners I likely never would have made my own. The result is that most of the fish I catch are on jigs I have poured or flies and spinners I have made. I get great enjoyment catching fish with my ties. I also like making them for others. In fact, many have asked me if I sell them. My answer is always "no". I'll give them away if I have extras but if I have to make them to sell, tying them would become work. I certainly don't want my hobby to become work.

I encourage each of you to allow your kayak to take you in new fishing directions. Be open to new techniques and new lures. Whether you make them yourself or buy them, tie one on.

A collection of my pond streamers.

46

Chapter 10
A weighty matter

As I head into my fourth year as a kayak angler I have become more aware of the various fishing kayaks produced by the major manufacturers. I like to stay abreast of kayak market developments and innovations. One thing I have noticed is that the major makers serving our hobby, Hobie, Native, Jackson, Ocean Kayak, etc. tend to add more plastic and more features to their boats each year. The result is that the same model may get heavier from year to year.

I've also noticed an evolution of many (certainly not all) kayak anglers. Worried about stability and having ample storage they purchase a very large kayak. Indeed, some of their choices are so large they have to trailer them to launch sites -- the immediate problem with that is that most car-top launch sites prohibit trailers. In addition to having to wrestle with an unwieldy boat, they eliminate themselves from many excellent fishing locales. That 80-pound kayak that grew to 90 or even a 100-pound beast with accessories actually becomes a white elephant, not used as much as originally anticipated by its owner. Eventually it adds to the supply of used fishing kayaks on the market as their owners seek to downsize. Check the "Tackle Shop" listings on Snaggedline.com. That's the portion of the popular kayak fishing forum where anglers can list their boats for sale. The majority of the kayak listings there are the heavier models.

I submit again that a far cheaper alternative than a heavy kayak is found near the sidewalk right outside the front door of most Bass Pro Shops. A small aluminum Jon boat is cheaper, more stable, has more storage room and is lighter in weight than many of the popular jumbo sized fishing kayaks.

I believe the tendency to produce heavier kayaks is a big mistake on behalf of the manufacturers. I purchased my Hobie Revo because at the time it was the lightest pedal kayak available. Yet it still weighs more than 60 pounds unfitted which is the upper limit of my capacity to car-top a kayak. I have helped my friends load their kayaks and I know for example I could not car-top an Outback by myself. Because of its width I would also have a hard time lifting the Slayer 10 by myself to my vehicle's roof, even though it has specified weight that is less than my Hobie.

My point is that as an older angler, sixty-plus years, the transportability of a kayak is a very important attribute to me. Because of that and looking ahead to a time when even my Revo becomes too heavy for me, I recently purchased a Native Ultimate 12 kayak as a second boat.

I broke convention in several ways by purchasing the Ultimate 12. First, it's a paddle kayak. Some may find that a regression since I started in the hobby with a pedal kayak. I make no dispute that a pedal kayak is an amazing fishing machine. At my present age I can still cover 12 or even 15 miles in a given day with the Revo. I know I won't be able to do that in the Ultimate. A second break with convention is that the Ultimate is not a Sit-On-Top kayak. It's more like a small canoe. It has no double hull and no scuppers to drain shipped water. Some might say that eliminates it from use on tidal waters. However, I have used Ultimates on guided kayak fishing trips to Tampa, Florida in high winds and choppy seas. It's a very seaworthy kayak. Nevertheless, there is no substitute for prudence and I will not tempt fate in a boat with no scuppers in big water locally.

But here's the real reason I purchased it. At a specified weight of only 49 pounds it's very light fishing kayak that is still large enough to have decent roominess and capacity and long enough to track straight.

I use it for small water trips to tidal creeks and freshwater ponds. It's pretty much stock with no additions or modifications. I carry only a few rods in it and it has no electronics. To me it is the essence of kayak fishing's roots – a simple paddle boat to get me closer to fish when wading or shore access is not feasible.

I find paddling a welcome change of pace from pedaling and I especially enjoy it in skinny water where I do not have to be concerned about grounding out my Mirage Drive fins. In fact, as I write this in 2016 I have taken my Ultimate on as many outings this season as my Revo. I thoroughly enjoy my time in it and most of all I appreciate the ease of loading it on my van at home and upon completion of my trips at the launch.

To summarize, I am not being critical of those who enjoy their large fishing kayaks. Those boats are excellent fishing platforms. Their owners are fortunate to have the youth and or strength to handle them. But I will say that there is a big difference between grappling 60 and 80 pounds and an even bigger difference between 80 and 100 pounds. In fact, a mere extra 5 pounds once you are near your practical weight limit can produce strained back muscles or a more serious injury that may prevent you from participating in a wonderful hobby you enjoy. My advice is to consider this "weighty matter" before you purchase a kayak or as you continue in the hobby with the addition of another boat to your fleet.

My Native Ultimate 12 – Comfortable and lightweight.
Photo courtesy of John Veil.

Chapter 11
Thoughts on trolling from an old troll

Without a doubt trolling is a technique that produces many sizable stripers for kayak anglers. It has certainly been that way for me. During my first kayak fishing year I avoided it. But as my time on the water increased I trolled more. At first I trolled only one rod at a time. I held the rod in my right hand as I pedaled, steering with my left. I landed a good number of fish that way and sizeable ones in the spring. When I purchased my BlackPak I configured it to hold two rods for trolling. Many of my friends troll four rods at once. I admire their tenacity and fervor but I have no desire to join them by trolling four lines. I frequently tangle my two lines. I do not know how they keep four lines from meeting in a macramé-like mess. But the fact remains that trolling produces lots of hookups. It also takes great skill to read the water and locate the fish. A fish finder is very handy for that because it will show you the structure, depth and channel edges where stripers cruise in their quest for food.

I will not delve deeply into the matter because the definitive kayak trolling bible has already been written by Alan Batista entitled, <u>Light Tackle Kayak Trolling on the Chesapeake Bay</u>. It's an outstanding treatise and I could never approach his expertise on the subject. John Veil also covers the topic extensively in his book, <u>Fishing in the Comfort Zone</u> with practical advice on tackle, techniques and what to look for on the water to optimize your trolling catches.

Trolling is a surprisingly simple concept. In effect you are dragging candy bars on a string through a kindergarten class. Just like those kids would not stay in their seats at the sight of the Hershey Bars pulled across their classroom floor, hordes of hungry stripers cannot contain their exuberance at the sight of your lures. If you get your bait within their spatial range and if that bait is similar in shape to the natural foods they are eating, you will more than likely end up with a fish on your line.

I approach the task very unscientifically. First, I rarely troll in waters deeper than 15 feet. That's because I carry no tackle on my kayak to reach below that depth. I usually put a ½ ounce jig head with a trailing plastic or buck tail on one rod and a similarly weighted crank bait or bucktail jig on the other. I cast them both behind my kayak (maybe 40 or 50 feet) and place the rods into their holders. Then I start pedaling. If I feel the lures dragging on the bottom, I either speed up my pedaling or I wind in some line until the lures clear the bottom. If I get no hits in areas I know hold fish, either because my buddies nearby are catching them or from the presence of schools on my fish finder, I pull in the lures and check them for fouling. If I am in an appropriately fishy area and not getting hit, I always check to see that there is no debris stuck to my lures. Even the tiniest piece of subaquatic vegetation clinging to a lure will discourage a fish from striking.

That's about the extent of my trolling preparation and technique. As artless as it sounds, it works as long as I am trolling areas that contain fish. That said, and simplicity aside, it's my least favorite form of kayak fishing. I know this is sacrilege here in the Chesapeake's kayak trolling kingdom.

There are three reasons I would rather cast than troll:

First, trolling is hard work. I've mentioned earlier in this book that I have travelled double digit miles on many outings. Invariably when I travel that far, I have been trolling. Even with my pedal kayak that's tiring. I recall once pedaling right past breaking fish on my way back to the launch after a particularly lengthy trolling trip. I was simply too tired to cast to the breakers. One more hookup wouldn't have mattered to me that day after catching so many stripers by tolling.

Alternately, I can launch into an area and travel maybe five or six miles roundtrip and still catch plenty of fish by targeting certain areas with either flies or conventional tackle. I find that much more relaxing. It also fits nicely with my fishing history of river wading and shooting lures and flies to likely fishy areas. It's a familiarity borne of my past and aided now by my kayak.

Second, I cannot escape the fact that I feel like I'm cheating when I troll. Here I am wandering miles in the Bay hoping to stumble across fish. Although I confine my search sites to reasonable trolling areas it's often still a surprise when I find them. It's a different intellectual process for me when I launch pinpoint casts to areas that I think should hold fish. I'm not surprised when I hook one lying next to riprap or downstream of the current behind a piling. I expect a fish to be there and it seems appropriately just in my mind to catch it. I found it by reason and logic and I had to make an accurate cast to catch it. I didn't stick my lure on the wood of the dock and I didn't lodge it into the crevices of the rock retaining wall. I believe I seriously earned that fish by correctly anticipating its presence and launching the perfect cast in its direction. When I troll I feel my catches are manna from heaven — gifts more than deserved rewards.

Third, trolling success can become routine, perhaps even too easy. I often catch two fish at once while trolling. My friends who troll four rods have contended with three or four fish on the line at once. And if you're with a group it's not unusual for each person to be hooked up simultaneously. It's not unheard of but it's a lot harder to make consecutive catches in the same area while casting, at least not in the same numbers that trolling produces.

By no means do I wish to detract from those who successfully troll. I readily admit I do not possess their tenacity or skill in reading the water and its subsurface terrain. But I'd like the readers to know that trolling is just one form of successful kayak fishing. If you're like me and your mind wanders while trolling; if you think a fish might be hanging on that distant breakwater while you're trolling thirty yards past it; or if you're simply tired of the constant expenditure of energy that trolling requires, give other forms of fishing from your kayak a try. Our plastic boats are amazingly adaptive tools for catching fish. Make sure you discover their full range of capabilities.

John Veil with a nice striper caught trolling in the Magothy River.

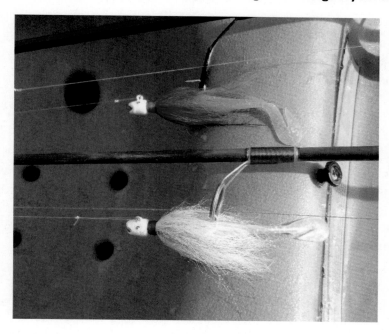

Your grandfather used them. Bucktails remain an effective trolling lure.

Chapter 12
Casting doubt away

Indeed, I often feel like the odd man out. I own a pedal kayak and trolling is not my preferred choice to fish. My favorite method is casting. It works just fine from a kayak. Certainly I do not put fish in the boat in the same numbers as those who troll, not usually anyway. Although, there have been days when my quantities were impressive.

I recall a session on the Severn when a particular stretch of riprap yielded 30 white perch in under an hour. I distinctly remember the number 30 because I vowed to myself I would stop when I reached that number. I could have caught more. In that instance the structure was to my left. I sat about 2 yards away from the riprap in 3 feet of water and slowly pedaled my Revo parallel to it. I cast one of my jig spinners about 30 feet ahead slightly to the left so that the lure dropped just in front of the rocks. I maintained a steady medium retrieve speed. The perch were thick and in a feeding mood. Darned near every cast along that wall produced a fish.

Action like that is exceptional. It's rare and it therefore becomes unforgettable. It's memorable because it's different than fishing a blitz where you see stripers feeding on the surface. In this case, even though I was in shallow water nothing revealed to me that the white perch were present. I saw no bait moving and certainly the perch were not surfacing.

Let me share a few techniques I used in the above situation that may help you find fish while casting:

- I cast with my right hand. That means it is easier for me to throw lures or flies to my left. That is why I set up my run along the riprap with the structure to my left. I do that whenever I can. Usually the only thing that will prevent me from setting up my preferred cast-to-the-left approach is a strong wind.

- I sat close to the riprap (6 feet) and cast ahead and slightly to my left. That meant my retrieve ran close and parallel to the structure. That kept my lure in front of the structure longer than if I had sat farther out and cast perpendicular to the riprap. If I had done that, strikes may have occurred close to the riprap but probably not after my lure got away from it. My lure would have been running through fishless water for much of the retrieve. Certainly the odds were greater that the perch were close to the riprap.

- I never cast straight over my bow. If I did, it wouldn't matter which direction I approach structure. As explained above I cast to the left of the bow most of the time because I am right handed. The reason I never cast straight ahead is because I have rods stored upright behind my seat. As long as I angle my cast, I cannot possibly hit those rods either with the rod in my hand or even with my extended fly line when fly casting. Note that I can throw backhanded casts to the right. But rarely will I cast to the right of the bow. It's awkward regardless of which kind of tackle I am using, spinning, bait casting or fly. Staying to the left is best for me.

- I used a proven lure in a likely spot. White perch find jig spinners hard to resist and riprap is a favorite white perch hangout in the summer. I expected to find white perch there. I did not expect to catch so many. But I would have been greatly surprised if I had not caught one. Additionally, stripers like spinners and often swim with white perch. On the run I described above no stripers interrupted my string of 30 perch. But I often do catch stripers and white perch side-by-side. I use a lure attractive to both species. (Note: Experience has taught me to pour my 1/8-ounce jig molds, the ones I turn into spinners, with heavier hooks. Sixteen inch Stripers and 20 inch pickerels can straighten a freshwater hook.)

- I moved while I was casting. I didn't sit anchored in place. It's interesting that pedal driven kayaks are deemed invaluable for trolling. I find my Revo perfect for casting because I am constantly moving while casting. I can move along a shoreline just like a professional bass angler in a Ranger Boat with his feet controlling his Minn Kota trolling motor. My hands are free to manipulate my fishing rod and my feet make me go forward just like the bass pro.

Structure in the above example was riprap. But it could have been a shaded area with heavy vegetation or point of shoreline jutting out into the water. I would still approach these areas from the left even if I had to pedal past them and turn around.

A legal striper caught with a 1/8 oz. jig spinner among white perch.

More challenging, especially in heavily wooded ponds and creeks are downed trees. They make wonderful bass and pickerel habitat. But sometimes because of terrain and close quarters, it is difficult to make a "dominant hand approach". In those cases, I make perpendicular casts in and among the branches. It's inevitable that you will lose lures or flies in downed trees. If you don't, you probably aren't getting close enough to the structure to entice a fish. Expect some losses – another benefit of making your own flies and lures.

Not all structure is visible from my kayak. Bottom variations such as ridges, holes or channels draw fish. Knowing where these underwater attractants are either aided by a fish finder or general knowledge will help to determine where to cast in what otherwise appears to be open non distinct water. This is typically how I fish in Tampa with the expert knowledge of a guide pointing out likely spots. Locally, I know where many of these bottom differences exist on my normal fishing routes.

Regardless of where I cast, I am an impatient angler. After two, three maybe four casts to a particular spot, I will move on if I catch no fish. Generally, I work from out to in. What I mean by that is my first cast may drop four feet from a stump. The next one will fall within two feet. And then I'll hit right beside the stump. When I catch fish I'll stay in that particular area and work it hard. Pickerel, perch, stripers and speckled trout can often be found on successive casts to the same area.

The physical act of casting is also something I enjoy. In Chapter 8, I mentioned that long fly casts are not needed in a kayak. But a rhythmic casting stroke is still essential even for shorter casts. When you have that good coordinated tempo, the line and fly flows precisely to where you want it, just short of a branch for example or to the base of piling and no farther. It's a wonderful feeling to be so in synch with your equipment.

I can get the same sense of achievement slinging a small jig spinner on my ultra-lite spinning rod with a quick flip of my wrist. The jig, aided by the wind resistant spinning blade sails through the air coming down for a landing like a parachute exactly where I want it. That's a good feeling made even better when a fish strikes it shortly thereafter. Similarly, there is something positive to be said for the feeling that comes when I use my thumb to feather a free flowing spool on a bait cast reel so that my lure plops down where I want it.

The cast is only the first half of my preferred fishing method. The retrieve is the second. That often takes intuition and a little guesswork. With the exception of cold water, I have yet to be able to predict any environmental factor that will foretell the response of fish on a given day. There are times fish want a quicker retrieve, and at other times, especially in cool water, they want it slow.

Regarding speed, it is almost impossible to pull a lure away from an active hungry fish. Years ago, I had the good fortune to fish on a guided trip with Bob Clouser, originator of the famous fly that bears his name. It was a warm June day on the Susquehanna River, not far from the infamous Three Mile Island. We were catching smallmouth bass using Clouser Minnows, of course. He observed my deliberation in stripping the line the back to the boat and succinctly said, "Speed it up. You can't pull it too fast." That advice holds for most warm water fishing situations. In colder water it often helps to retrieve your lures slowly. You always need to be aware of your retrieves and if you're not getting strikes, change up speeds just like a major league pitcher. You want to entice those fish just like the pitcher wants to fool the batter into swinging.

For top water, short of a striper feeding blitz where any approach will work, including letting the lure sit still, sometimes subtle movements out catch more vigorous popping actions. In those cases, either moving a popper slowly or switching to a slider type of fly which smoothly dives and returns to the surface is the key to success. The only way to know is to try both approaches.

My main point about casting is that it is not just flailing lures or flies hit or miss. Well, actually it is. But so are all forms of fishing -- trolling, netting or using bait. There's truth to the saying, "That's why they call it fishing, not catching". Absolutely, the vast majority of my casts come up devoid of fish. Compare that to the miles trollers travel while not catching fish. We definitely are hooked by an imperfect hobby to continue to pursue it with the odds stacked against us. But I find that the physical act of casting provides intrinsic value. For me the cast itself, laid out perfectly, is the catch, not the fish.

Casting is therefore a viable alternative to the more popular trolling for catching fish from your kayak.   While many anglers are attracted to the pedals in Hobies and Natives (and more brands each year) for trolling, those kayaks are great platforms for the precise positioning I described above to enhance your casts.   In fact, Native pedal kayaks can go in reverse which is often helpful in quiet waters for retrieving lures hung up in branches or for subtly backing out to get needed distance for a strategic cast.

If I haven't convinced you with my examples, I can only suggest that you give casting a try and see for yourself. I think if you do you will indeed cast all doubt away about its utility in kayak fishing.

Riprap in the Severn. A great place to cast.

Eastern Shore pond – Toss a popper under that log for a hungry bass.

Vegetation at the waterline and shade – An ideal casting target.

Chapter 13
To paddle or pedal, that is the question

I am fortunate to own two kayaks, a Hobie Revolution 13 and Native Ultimate 12. The former is pedal driven and the latter is paddle powered. Each of my boats is relatively light with trim lines compared to most fishing kayaks. Both glide easily through the water and both are joy to ride in. While they are each seaworthy and somewhat interchangeable with respect to where I fish with them, I find they suit different angling styles for me and each functions better in different weather conditions.

My pedal driven Hobie is a high performance kayak. It's fast yet surprisingly stable given its slim lines. It slices through waves and wind with its sharp bow and low profile. It is a great boat for crossing open Bay waters either to fish along the way by trolling or to travel to distant tributaries. It's easy to pedal ten or more miles in a single 3 to 4-hour fishing session with my Hobie.

The major advantage of a pedal driven kayak for most anglers is that pedaling is a more efficient way to move a kayak through the water than paddling. Leg muscles are stronger and more resilient than arm muscles in repetitive activity. Those who pedal, generally, are able to travel farther and longer without rest than those who paddle. That's why pedal driven kayaks are favored by those who like to troll. That does not mean that those in pedal kayaks will out-catch those in paddle driven kayaks. I've witnessed some herculean accomplishments by anglers trolling in paddle kayaks, traveling just as far or farther than their friends in pedal driven kayaks and catching more fish. But the fact remains that pedal-powered kayakers generally give themselves more opportunities to catch fish than their paddling friends simply because they often cover more water.

Most pedal kayakers and paddle kayakers who troll use rod holders. Therefore, neither enjoys an advantage in how rods are secured in their kayaks. But a big advantage for pedal power is that anglers' hands are unencumbered to immediately attend to fish hooked on line.   Pedal kayakers don't have to stop paddling and stow the paddle before grabbing the rod with the fish on it. Additionally, at hookup pedals actually help to land fish. Pedal driven kayak anglers can:

- Maintain forward motion while using their hands to reel in the fish.
- Keep pressure on the hooked fish while simultaneously moving forward and reeling in their empty lines to avoid tangling them and then begin fighting fish.
- Turn toward the fish while simultaneously moving forward and reeling it in. By that I mean if the hooked fish is on the right side of their kayak, turning their boat to the right will keep the fish from crossing any lines they still have out to the left. That gives the fish less opportunity to cross (tangle with) other line(s) if they are trolling two or more rods.

I also suggest that pedal driven kayaks generally counter strong winds better than paddle powered kayaks. The reason for that is that you can maintain constant propulsion underwater with either with fins (Hobie Mirage Drive) or a propeller (Native Propel). At the same time, you can continuously compensate for wind-drift with your rudder.

I recall an occasion when I was paddling a Native Ultimate 14.5 in a heavy port side wind that arose late in the afternoon. Winds gradually grew and remained steady between 15 and 20 mph. The Ultimate 14.5 has a tendency depending on the load it is carrying to turn its bow into the wind. The wind pushes against the stern and causes the bow to pivot in the opposite direction. The only way I could both go forward and maintain a straight line was to paddle exclusively with my left arm. That was exhausting. I have never experienced such a bow drift in my Hobie despite being in similar windy conditions.

However, there are drawbacks to pedaling. Generally, pedal kayaks weigh more than similarly sized or even longer paddle kayaks. My Revo weighs 13 pounds more than my Ultimate despite being only a foot longer. The pedal mechanism, the Mirage Drive, has many moving parts and is subject to damage and wear and tear. In additional to the emergency on-water repair I described in Chapter 7, I have had to replace a pulley and cable on my Mirage Drive. The Mirage Drive is also something extra to carry, and added weight in the kayak and it must be protected while in use to avoid grounding out or hitting underwater objects.

Having started with a pedal kayak and using it exclusively for over a year, I was concerned about trying a paddle kayak. Using pedals is so easy I was apprehensive about paddling. Would I have the stamina for paddling during a full day's fishing?

My first extensive kayak paddling experience was on a trip to Tampa, Florida with a kayak fishing guide. It was there that I was introduced to Native Ultimate kayaks. I thoroughly enjoyed the experience. Paddling was so much more basic than pedaling and I felt more connected to the movement of the kayak than I do while pedaling my Hobie. Yes, it required more personal exertion but not excessively so. Mind you we did no trolling. But we still traveled over eight miles according to the guide, with ample time anchored and casting for fish in between paddling sessions. Given that moderate pace, I was very pleased because I knew I could have paddled considerably longer.

A paddle kayak is simple to operate. It's generally lighter and easier to get to the water than a pedal driven kayak. It draws less water because there is no propulsion mechanism hanging beneath the hull. Unless you also have a rudder, the only moving part is the paddle. That means there is less mechanical paraphernalia to set up at the launch site. There also is usually more room on the deck because there are no pedals to contend with.

I made a case in Chapter 12 that pedal driven kayaks are great for various casting scenarios, especially when you are working close to shorelines. I stand by that. But there are times when a paddle kayak is more convenient. Fishing tight to docks and piers is one example where a paddle kayak is preferable. It is easier to pivot for a sharp turn away from a piling in a paddle kayak than with a pedal kayak which generally requires a large turning radius. Working among down trees is also easier with a paddle kayak. Invariably you will get your lure snagged in branches. It is easier to go in among the branches to retrieve it by paddling than pedaling. Note that Native's Propel kayaks offer reverse which is helpful in backing out of such situations as long as the drive is not obstructed by underwater branches. Getting over shallow sandbars and other obstacles underwater is also easier in a paddle kayak.

In short, a paddle kayak is a wonderful fishing platform. It's great for up-close angling – creeks, ponds and any situation where you work tight to structure. But paddle powered kayaks also serve others well in open water scenarios for trolling. You can fish in a paddle kayak alongside of your peddle driven friends.

It may be a matter of economics. Paddle kayaks are more affordable. My Revo retailed for almost twice as many dollars as my Ultimate 12. That makes the choice easy for some. But for others it's situational. I use my Native for quick trips or when I feel like paddling, especially in smaller waters. It's great for outings when I travel light, carrying only one or two rods. On a paddle trip I am more likely to be targeting one species or practicing one fishing style. I am less apt to change my fishing technique during a paddle trip, to go from trolling to casting, for example. I like the ease of paddle kayak angling. I can set up in a flash at the launch site and be on my way. It's almost the same as when I choose to fly fish. I paddle when I want that tactile sense of being one with the water, of being captive to its current and as close to wading as I can get without actually stepping into the water.

The answer to the question posed by the title of this chapter is, "It depends." Cost, personal goals, the situation and your preferences matter. It's largely up to you. To paddle or pedal – the best approach is how you decide to kayak fish based on those four factors. There is no best way.

Paddling or…

…pedaling. It depends.

Chapter 14
The dreaded skunk

Pepe Le Pew, zippo, nada, nothing...the skunk happens. There are days when you simply cannot put a fish in your kayak. It's especially frustrating to be part of a group outing and to be the low guy on the catch tally, especially when your contribution is zero. But it will happen to you. It happens to all kayak anglers eventually.

While I believe happenstance can be a leading reason, I also believe it can be self-induced. I know I have been the primary cause of the condition on a number of occasions. My guilt can mostly be traced to my wanderlust. I often commit the sin of leaving fish to catch fish. Recall my comments about trolling. I am constantly looking at likely fishy spots even while I am trolling through a school of hungry fish. I'm non-repentant on this matter. What else can I say?

Additionally, I think my Revo contributes to my desire to travel because it moves so easily with minimal effort. I can point it into the wind and waves and slice through them freely to go off on my own. Sometimes I do that to my detriment in terms of fish count. But the journey is sure fun.

Another cause of poor catching is failing to heed what the fish are telling you with their behavior. If your buddies are chattering on channel 68 that they're boating stripers with white 4 inch paddletails in five to ten feet of water and you continue to troll a blue Rat-L-Trap in 15 feet with no hits, the fault for minimal catches is yours.

Even if you discount the successes of your friends to chance, if you make no adjustments on the water when the bite is slow the fault is yours. Your changes can be anything – a new location, a different lure, or altering speeds on your retrieving or trolling. Anything that modifies your approach may help. To do nothing different only guarantees your results will be the same.

Seasonal patterns can also fool us, especially early in a given season. You may have heard reports of yellow perch runs or the early arrival of stripers in a Chesapeake tributary.   Or you may hear that the fall top water bite is on.   Yet when you get to the well-publicized site, you are blanked.   Early season announcements by anglers who happened to find a windfall are perhaps the cruelest of all reports.   The bite they experienced rarely lasts and certainly, its location is tenuous at best. Many kayak anglers anxious to get on the water forget that fish have fins and they swim. Fish move around a lot especially before a given location is choked with their particular species during a migratory run. It's best to curb your expectations at the beginning of such migrations. If catching fish is the absolutely the most important thing to you, you may want to save yourself disappointment by fishing according to the calendar of experience – March for yellow perch, April for spring stripers, May for largemouth bass and so on.

Some anglers are fortunate to have intuition.   I am not one of them. I believe I am a fairly good fisherman but experience and observation have been my teachers.   There is not one thing about angling I surmised on my own that came true. What I know about kayak angling comes from my experience in fishing with others who are vastly better anglers than me and who graciously shared their knowledge with me.   I'm a good learner. But I'm not one to develop techniques on my own. That means I am at a distinct disadvantage when the bite is hard. Once my menu of known tactics is exhausted I usually am physically spent and it is time for me to leave the water.   But others have intuition and use it to find fish when people like me cannot. Accept it. You either have that sixth angling sense or you do not.

Sometimes it is less frustrating to catch no fish than to catch just a few. One season I got off to an extremely slow start. On every early outing I caught just one or two fish. I was fishing mostly for pickerel late in the winter.   It was well prior to the normal spring migrations of various species further reducing my catch chances.   Given the finicky nature of cold water pickerels I guess I should have been pleased. But others fishing with me were not stuck in the one or two fish rut. It was so predictable that I should have immediately returned to the launch after my first fish of the day because I was doomed to cast fruitlessly thereafter. I tried every on-the-water adjustment I could think of except for using live minnows for bait. However, the situation corrected itself before long. The water got warmer as the season progressed and the fish got more active. Sometimes you just have to wait for the right moment.

My last thought on the matter concerns luck. Thomas Jefferson said, "I'm a great believer in luck, and I find the harder I work the more I have of it." That quote substantiates the popular impression most historians have of Jefferson as a man who believed in preparation and labored long for perfection in many endeavors. Hence we have a beautifully worded Declaration of Independence thanks to his pen. We have his magnificent homestead in Monticello to admire as an architectural delight. And the University of Virginia exists thanks to his vision and labor. But I would also venture to say that Jefferson was no fisherman. If he was he would not have equated hard work with good luck. There are days when no matter how many casts you make, no matter how many miles you troll and no matter how well you match the hatch, you are not going to succeed in bringing fish to the boat. The fish are going to have lockjaw, ignoring perfectly placed casts. Who can explain why? Or they are going to shimmy off your hook if you do manage to interest one to bite. You might think a coming weather front has put the fish down. Or you may believe your hook was dull or the fact that you de-barbed it is why you lost the fish. Yet the same hook worked well on other days. I submit the only explanation for these examples of angling injustice is bad luck. When no other explanation will suffice blame it on bad luck.

The good news is that angling misfortunate can change in a heartbeat, indeed on your very next cast. And isn't that what keeps us coming back for more even after we experience the humiliation of a skunky outing?

Chapter 15
Sleeping in a bear's den

I mentioned earlier that finding good fishing partners is very important. It's like choosing the correct spouse. Get a bad one and your trip/life can be miserable. The "four Cs" of conversation, congeniality, compatibility and camaraderie are especially important on overnight fishing trips when you share close quarters for a number of days. But as I am about to explain another critically important factor can trump the "four Cs".

Over the years, I've been on many fishing excursions from wading rivers for smallmouth bass in Maine to kayaking for speckled trout in Florida. Each of them was enjoyable in spite of the occasional times when finicky fish or troublesome weather interrupted the fun. But it was on an otherwise fine largemouth bass trip to Pennsylvania I learned another valuable lesson in picking fishing buddies.

I rented a cabin in a Pennsylvania state park for five days of fishing and invited two co-workers. It was a long anticipated trip, endlessly discussed at the office coffee mess and the subject of many workplace emails. I now shudder to think of the workplace productivity lost due to that trip.

The cabin was nicely appointed with a kitchen, living room, bathroom, two bedrooms and fully furnished. There were three of us on the trip. We each chose bunks in the bedrooms upon arrival. I decided to share a room with George, not his real name. I tossed my sleeping bag on a bunk and headed to the lake for an afternoon session with the bass. The bass were in a pre-spawn pattern, easy to find and wiling to bite. It was a good afternoon made even better by a grilled dinner of burgers and brats at the cabin. There was lively discussion at the table, beer and wine and lots of laughter and a campfire to boot. It was a fine start to the trip.

Just before bedtime each of us shared strategies and boldly predicted the rude awakening we would give those largemouth bass at dawn. It had been a long day of travel, unpacking and fishing and I was tired. I fell off to sleep quickly.

Then it happened, the moment when I knew it would be a long week. At first I thought it was a dream. I heard a deep rumbling sound typically associated with heavy machinery moving earth. As my eyes opened in the darkness I momentarily thought I was back in California where on a recent work trip I had been in an earthquake. There was an unforgettable reverberating noise in my hotel room that night as the foundation of the high-rise Holiday Inn tremored in the quake. I startled to full consciousness to realize I wasn't in Long Beach, California. I was near York, Pennsylvania in a lakeside cabin. What in the world was I hearing? There was another guttural echo. There aren't any bears near York, Pennsylvania I thought. Or maybe there are. That's it. There must be a bear outside my window!

Of course there was no bear. It was George. In the otherwise stillness of the night the resonances emanating from his nose and mouth seemed to have the decibel range of a Boeing 747 at takeoff. I tried to cope. I lay there in desperation and sought to will myself back to sleep. But it was impossible. George had a perfect cadence underway, his lengthy wind tunnel-like tours of rushing air ending with a sonic boom of nostril inflection. After each grating growl I could count to three and another decibel shattering utterance would start. Soon the anticipation of each of George's thunderous exhalations was driving me crazy.

I reached down to the floor and grabbed my shoe. I threw a fastball at George, hitting him squarely on the shoulder. "Stop snoring," I said in a whisper. Why I bothered to whisper made no sense. There was nothing subtle about his part in this saga. No doubt the bullfrogs in the lake were worried that they were about to lose their harems to the "frogzilla" they heard near our cabin. Nevertheless, after my shoe struck him his rhythm broke...for one three-count cycle. He didn't even wake up. Then he was back at it, louder than before.

I couldn't stand it anymore. I grabbed my sleeping bag and stumbled out to the living the room. I tossed my bag on the sofa. Unfortunately, it covered Al, my other co-worker on the trip. He grunted to consciousness when my bag tumbled on top of him.

"What are you doing out here?" I asked him.

"I heard that damned racket in my room through the wall," he said.

"Geez, I can still hear it out here," I said.

"You'll get used to it," he replied.

"How in the hell does his wife sleep?" I wondered out loud.

Without a second's hesitation Al said, "I'll bet she's sleeping pretty good tonight."

I laid my bag on the living room floor and tried to nod off. But I still could not fall asleep. Even though the decibel level had dropped significantly I could still hear each of George's trumpet calls through the knotty pine walls. At that point it wasn't as much the noise as the expectation of another annoying blast that kept me awake.

I left the living room and moved to the kitchen floor. My legs were partially under the dining table because the kitchen was rather small. I could still hear each explosion from my co-worker in his cave. Now my mind was starting to play tricks. I thought the cups and saucers in the cupboards were rattling with each detonation from George's room. I knew my only salvation was outside. Once again I grabbed my sleeping bag and I headed to my F-150 truck. It had a cap on the cargo bed. It was merely a matter of clearing some of my tackle to find a place to sleep. At last, with a long driveway to shield me from George I heard only the soothing songs of katydids in the trees and I fell asleep. Thank goodness I had my truck on that trip. To this day I remember that F-150 fondly not for the many miles of trouble-free service it gave me but for the decent nights of slumber it provided me on my Pennsylvania fishing trip.

I must say my outings of late with my kayaking friends have not been hazardous to a good night's rest. Perhaps the cardiovascular workout of kayaking promotes sound sleeping habits. I've had excellent restful trips with my fellow kayak anglers. They include guided outings in Tampa, Florida and drivable destinations in nearby Virginia and Delaware. Whether camping in state parks or staying overnight in hotels, the only thing I ask of my fishing roommate is this: "Do you snore?" Fortunately, the answer has been "no" and my actual experience has proven that to be true. I have not slept in a bear's den since that long ago Pennsylvania fishing trip and I hope I never do again.

John Rentch tends the grill on a great overnight kayak fishing trip at Trap Pond State Park, Delaware – An annual tradition for the OGWLF.

Chapter 16
The Severn again and again

It's great to get away and fish distant locations. The excitement of the planning, the packing, the travel and the day of arrival are all facets of the trip that I much anticipate. But it's also nice to have a marvelous fishing location so close to home. The Severn River is that place for me.

I have lived in Anne Arundel County, Maryland within 15 miles of the banks of the Severn for each of my 60 plus years of life. Yet I never wet a fishing line in the Severn until I got my kayak. I had no idea what an amazing fishery it was until my kayak granted me access to its heretofore inaccessible shorelines.

Without a doubt, Anne Arundel County has provided kayak anglers an invaluable asset in the form of Jonas Green Park. Located at the foot of the Route 450 U. S. Naval Academy (USNA) Bridge on the shore of the river, Jonas Green offers kayak anglers one of the best launching sites in the entire mid-Bay region. It has ample parking, is safe and clean, is patrolled by rangers and has a large sandy beach to launch from. Best of all there is no entry fee to the park, although access is limited to daylight hours. There is no boat ramp and trailers are not permitted; therefore, a cart is advisable for most kayak anglers to reach the water from the parking area.

And once you get to the water your fishing choices are many. There are well marked oyster beds on both shorelines between the USNA Bridge and the Route 50 Bridge to the north. At roughly one half of a mile wide, the Severn provides ample room to troll for stripers between the bridges, especially over or near those beds. While the main channel of the river can reach 25 to 30 feet deep the river edges are often only five to ten feet deep. The shorelines between the bridges provide various forms of structure from piers and pilings to riprap. There are areas of phragmites, or reeds that grow right to the waterline. Each of those forms of structure holds white perch and stripers in season. I can spend hours per each outing working flies and lures along the river edges between the bridges.

Also accessible are various tidal ponds between the bridges and north of the Route 50 Bridge. Each pond holds a healthy population of pickerels and white perch. It's not uncommon to run into a striper looking for an easy meal in those ponds. The only difficulty you may encounter, especially those with heavier kayaks is getting your boat into those ponds at low tide. Sometimes I can float into them but often I have to get out and drag my boat over exposed bottom to get in. But once in the fishing is usually worth the trouble.

From Jonas I can also reach several Severn creeks. The closest is College Creek which winds its way through the USNA, past the Academy cemetery on the right and various academic buildings on the left. Shortly after you pass those landmarks you will find yourself surrounded by undeveloped shorelines wooded to the waterline. It's hard to believe you are in the city of Annapolis. The view is more akin to a country setting. Only the Westminster clock chimes from a nearby church remind you that you are in a city.

On the same side of the river as College Creek, but north near the Route 50 Bridge is Weems Creek. Again, as you go farther back into the creek the shorelines get more rustic. Even in the populated area of the creek the houses are not closely spaced as they are on the Magothy River, for example. That means you can find plenty of unobstructed shoreline between houses.

Two destinations across the river from Jonas Green, but certainly reachable by kayak are Cove of Cork and Luce Creek. They are shorter in length than College and Weems Creeks but no less productive. Again, pickerel, white perch stripers and even pumpkinseeds are common catches in these locales.

If bigger water is to your liking, you can head south from Jonas Green toward Greenbury Point, the mouth of the Severn and the Bay itself. As you leave the beach and cross under the USNA Bridge give a wide berth to the fisherman using the pier at Jonas Green. You don't want to interfere with their lines or you will hear some choice words. Once past the USNA Bridge the Academy athletic field will be to your right.

I've seen lots of interesting activities on that field while traversing and fishing that part of the river. One summer day I was having success with schoolie stripers just south of the USNA Bridge. I was both casting a little and trolling a little. The fish were pretty thick and they weren't difficult to catch. Frankly I was more interested in the activities on shore. The plebes were getting a serious physical workout. They were running laps, doing calisthenics and in one particularly brutal activity they were in groups of 8 or 10 carrying telephone pole-length logs. They were literally running laps around the field carrying logs. I was exhausted just watching them.

After the log drill the plebes disappeared from the field. I figured they were getting a well-deserved rest so I headed back up river toward the USNA Bridge. When I got past the retaining wall for the athletic field I heard shouts of "stroke, stroke, stroke" from a megaphone. To my left, coming from the short stretch of beach on the Academy side of the river behind the retaining wall was a small armada of black rubber rafts. A group of plebes was lining the edges of each raft rowing with little paddles in cadence to the encouraging shouts from the megaphone. The problem was that I was directly in their path. I quickly cranked in my lure and pumped my Revo's pedals as fast as I could. I managed to get out of their way, just barely. I could hear the plebes huffing and puffing as they passed within a few yards of me on their way across the river. I'm glad I did not become a casualty in their training activity. Although I'm sure it would have made interesting reading in the resulting incident report – "Plebes swamp senior kayaker in Severn". Anyway, Academy life is vigorous for the Middies. I'm glad I view it from afar seated in my kayak.

As you progress toward the Bay you'll pass the USNA mooring area on the left side of the river for its Yard Patrol (YP) Boats. You should always be alert for boat traffic on the water, especially on the Severn. But you have to be especially vigilant in this area of the river because YP Boats are frequently out and about in various training activities. I joke with my buddies that there could be a farm boy from Nebraska at the helm who has never been on the water before! I always give YP Boats a lot of space. Despite the water I yield I've gotten toots of caution from them on occasion as I head to Greenbury Point, one of my favorite areas to fish.

If the Severn has a problem, it is wind. The river flows southeast into the Bay from its source. A strong prevailing double digit wind from the northwest can send large building waves down river right into the beach at Jonas Green. If I see conditions like that I do not tempt fate. There are other places I can go to get out of the wind. But if the wind is mostly from the east or the west, you can usually find a protected shoreline on the Severn to fish.

The Severn is definitely my preferred place to kayak fish. It's close to my house, access is easy, it's scenic, and there are a lot of interesting things going on in it and on its banks. Best of all it's full of fish catchable by a variety of methods. It's also pretty much open to fishing year-round thanks to willing pickerels that bite all winter long. That's I why I visit the Severn River again and again with my kayak.

The launch at Jonas Green.

76

A northwest wind at the end of a trip.

Typical scenery in a Severn creek.

Chapter 17
Bridging east

The Severn River offers proximity and excellent fishing for me. Even with Route 2 congestion and nine annoying traffic lights, I can usually get there within 30 minutes of departing my driveway. But if I drive only another 15 minutes, a completely different fishing environment awaits. All I have to do is cross the Governor William Preston Lane Jr. Memorial Bridge, more commonly known as the Bay Bridge. The landscape on the other side of the bridge quickly changes into the flat agrarian terrain of Maryland's Eastern Shore. It is like visiting another state. The Eastern Shore is always capitalized in print which adds to its identity as a separate geographic entity. In fact, more than once its political leaders have discussed seceding from Maryland. I'm glad it has not. It's a jewel for Marylanders and for me a relatively close fishing destination.

My preferred tidal destination when I cross the bridge is Goodhands Creek Landing. This site was first shared with me by Harry Steiner, one of the OGWLF, and a fellow fly fisherman. He characterized it as a place that simultaneously offers shelter from the wind and big water opportunities if you are so inclined. He could not have been more correct. The launch site is administered by Queen Anne's County. A daily or annual permit is required to use the launch. It's well worth the nominal fee because the Goodhands landing ramp provides kayak access to the some of the prettiest water and countryside imaginable. It's classic Eastern Shore tidal water.

As you come out of the creek and head south you'll approach Prospect Bay. The western shoreline along this path is largely natural with downed wood, phragmites reeds and sod banks with lots of cuts and inlets to explore. To the east is Hog Island, an excellent windbreak and a fish magnet, particularly the southeast side of the island. I have fished out of

Goodhands Creek for each of the CBKA Tournaments I have participated in and each of my contest entries have been caught near Hog Island.

In just the few years I have had my kayak I have seen Chesapeake Bay erosion first-hand at Hog Island. I recall when there was a small trickle of water cutting the island from north-to-south. I watched that trickle of water grow in width in succeeding years. Now I can traverse it in my kayak which means Hog Island is presently in reality two islands.

Sod banks at Goodhands.

I have caught stripers, white perch and even channel catfish at Goodhands. But there is another species that pays a visit to this area in droves in the late spring and early summer – cow nose rays. These docile members of the shark family are the bane of kayak anglers throughout the Bay but something about Goodhands Creek and Prospect Bay is particularly intriguing to them. It's not unusual to see massive schools of them gliding throughout these waters.

Catching a ray is inevitable if you kayak fish in the Bay long enough. At first you are exhilarated by the hookup. You know you have caught something big from the sheer pressure on the end of your line. But then you don't feel that familiar head shake of a large striper and your heart sinks. You realize you have hooked a ray and your next thought is how to get rid of it. Otherwise you are in for a long pull and if you do get the ray to the gunnels of your kayak, you surely will be soaked as it repeatedly thrashes near your hull. You might even get stung by the toxic spike at the base of its tail. That was a fate suffered by Captain John Smith 400 years ago as he explored the Chesapeake. In fact, the sting from a cow nose ray also almost killed him. So sure were his men that their captain was going to perish that they dug his grave. But he pulled through the infection to everyone's surprise, including his own.

When I catch a cow nose ray, my first thought is to get rid of it, even if that means sacrificing my lure. I point my rod directly at the ray so there is no pressure on my guides or the rod itself. I put my hand over the spool of my spinning reel to prevent the drag from engaging. Note that if I am using baitcasting gear I use my thumb to stop the drag. And then I pull back and wait for the forward progress of the ray to break my leader. Freed of the brute and minus my Rat-L-Trap or jig I tie on another lure and keep fishing.

However, some kayak anglers relish a good tussle with a cow nose ray. I witnessed such a battle, an epic contest, near the waters of Goodhands Creek. A cow nose ray versus a kayak -- Moby-Dick versus Captain Ahab's ship The Pequod. In both scenarios there was a determined angler and a beast from the deep with a tremendous desire to be free from the confines imposed on it by man. The clash I observed even lasted nearly as long as Hollywood's version of Herman Melville's famous tale. Assuming Gregory Peck's lead role of Captain Ahab was none other than my good friend Terry.

I was fishing near the southwest edge of Hog Island fan-casting the surrounding waters for stripers. I saw a dark cloud in the water off to my left. It was a school of cow nose rays swimming toward Prospect Bay.

The tips of their wing-like fins flashed above the water and I could see their brown backs glistening a few inches under the surface in the sunlight. My lure was directly in their path. Having tangled with them before and wanting to avoid a repeat performance I cranked in my line as fast I as I could to avoid any potential for a hook-up. I succeeded. My lure was safely dangling from my rod tip and hanging over the bow of my kayak as I watched the procession of rays pass me on their way toward Prospect Bay – where Terry was fishing 200 to 300 yards away.

Had this happened in subsequent years I would have radioed Terry and warned him about the oncoming herd. But this was before either of us had a radio. All I could do was sit there and watch. It was like a World War II movie where a submarine commander targets an enemy battleship. He stares into the periscope and coolly delivers navigational orders and coordinates to his crew and then he shouts, "Fire one! Fire two!" The scene invariably shifts to torpedoes speeding through the water on their deadly mission toward a distant unsuspecting target. I watched those rays swim en masse toward an unsuspecting Terry. I waited. I saw his rod tip rise and I heard his squeal of exuberance when he hooked one, the sound delayed from when I observed the movement of his rod tip due to the distance that separated us. Terry was hooked up but I knew before he did that he did not have the big striper he had hoped on the end of his line. That is how the battle began.

I don't know when Terry realized what he had. The first impression always is that you have latched onto the striper of a lifetime. But the line doesn't zip from your reel when you stick a ray. It's more like the sustained pull of a tug-of-war contest. You gain a little and you give a little. There is no distinctive head shake to vibrate your rod tip that reveals a striper has taken your lure. Instead there is a constant pressure as the fish slowly takes off pulling you along for the ride. A ray will give you a slow motion version of the famous "Nantucket sleigh ride."

That was the situation when I arrived on the scene together with others in our fishing group. Soon Terry was widely circled by a group of kayak anglers watching him just like many of us had done in our school days when two kids decided to settle their dispute with their fists on the playground after the dismissal bell rang. Some shouted encouragement. Others laughed. I yelled, "Cut the line!"

Terry wouldn't consider that. He wanted to land the ray and most important, he wanted his lure back. Having donated many $4.95 Rat-L-Traps to rays in my brief kayak fishing history, I knew that was a fruitless goal. I watched our circle of kayaks yield space to Terry as the ray broke from its school on its quest for freedom. Evidently it wanted to go to the Chester River, some distance to the north because that's the general direction Terry's kayak headed. Occasionally it would circle back in a large arc but mainly it headed north with Terry applying pressure from his end of the struggle trying desperately to gain line on the ray.

Had I been at the movies I would have been relaxing in my seat, well into my popcorn at this point in the story. But I was in a beautiful tidal area with willing stripers and white perch in the shallows. I really didn't want to watch Moby-Dick especially when I knew how the story would end. I wanted to fish. So I left the "theater" to glance only occasionally in Terry's direction as he and the ray dodged crab boats on their slow voyage north. From afar I would see splashes near his kayak as he got the brutish fish close time after time. Then the water would be calm around him as the ray got a burst of energy and broke away from its plastic captor. Lengthy periods of slow forward progress would follow as the two crept toward Kent Narrows. All the while Terry had his rod tip held high. It was nearly an hour into the battle and I was on the north side of Hog Island where I continued to fish while keeping an eye on my traveling companion as he and his ray circled the south side of the concrete breakwater wall. The ray then decided to turn toward the Kent Narrows Bridges and of course Terry followed. I saw him go under the first bridge and lost sight of him.

The ray had pulled Terry nearly two miles by this point in their memorable match. Both were reaching legendary status among the kayak anglers who witnessed the epic encounter. I wondered how much pressure his braided line and monofilament leader could sustain after an hour and fifteen minutes of steady tension. As it turned out, his line was near the breaking point because shortly after the ray pulled Terry past the second bridge in The Narrows the leader snapped. The ray was free and while he probably didn't realize it so was Terry.

I don't remember how many fish I caught during Terry's long dance with the ray. But I do know I would rather catch only one fish for an hour and fifteen minutes than tug on a cow nose ray for that same amount of time. However, Terry's stature grew among our kayak angling community with that catch. Even now, years after that marathon struggle when one of the OGWLF members hooks a ray, the common refrain is "Where's Terry when you need him?"

Cow nose rays aside, the reason I like Goodhands is because of the variety of fishing it offers. In addition to excellent structure along its banks and nearby Kirwan creek to explore on days when I need protection from high winds there are large areas of open waters of moderate depth good for kayak trolling. Also, I can easily reach Kent Narrows from the Goodhands launch and if I am particularly ambitious I can go all the way to the Chester River. It's an incredibly scenic area with an abundance of fish. Rarely am I disappointed with my outings to Goodhands.

Kayak fishing of a far different kind is also accessible when I trek across the Bay Bridge. Wye Mills, Tuckahoe and Unicorn are three Eastern Shore mill ponds that offer excellent opportunities for largemouth bass, bluegills, pickerel and crappie. Each is a small pond between 19 and 50 acres and each has free public access. If I venture to Laurel, Delaware, the 90-acre Trap Pond awaits. All four are classic mature mill ponds, shallow with downed wood and lily pads for structure. They offer a quiet contrast to fishing the tidal waters of the Bay. Turtles enjoying the sun are prevalent on logs even in March and bald eagles often circle overhead. Tuckahoe in particular has beaver houses and evidence of their work on shore with small tree stumps sharpened like pencils sticking out of the ground.

Because these ponds are so shallow, none is deeper than 8 feet, I often work my fly rod exclusively on my visits. I work the perimeters tossing poppers or steamers close to the shoreline or into the downed tree branches. I've never caught particularly big largemouth bass in these ponds but the action is fairly steady and the bass put up a nice fight on the fly. Far more action is often provided by bluegills, especially when they are nesting. They cannot ignore a rubber spider pattern or a small popper. There is little finesse in catching them. I don't even have to twitch the fly. I just let it float and the bluegills attack it with ferocity. The bluegills in these ponds are beautiful fish with deep orange bellies and dark purplish blue sides, probably due to the tannin in the water. Largemouth bass are actually members of the sunfish family along with bluegills. But I've often thought that if a bass fought like a bluegill they would be exhausting to catch. The really big bluegills turn their bodies sideways as you pull them in. The resistance they produce is significant – like your first paddle strokes from a dead stop.

On the last day of 2015, the OGWLF determined to send the year out on a good note, did an Eastern Shore "pond hop." The three Maryland ponds I mentioned are relatively close to each other. It is possible to fish all three in a single day and certainly easy to fish one in the morning and another afternoon. That is what did on December 31st. Unseasonably warm temperatures in the 50s enticed us to the water. We stopped first at Wye Mills and then continued to Tuckahoe. The fish did not disappoint as we caught quite a few bass and crappie among us. Oddly we did not catch any pickerels that day and that is the species that we thought would be most active. Nevertheless, it was a great way to end our fishing calendar year.

Bridging east is one of my favorite kayak angling activities. Whether drifting along the sod banks at Goodhands Creek or floating on a tranquil mill pond I am never disappointed by the scenery nor by the fish attracted to my offerings.

Typical vegetation in an Eastern Shore pond.

Bald cypress trees in Delaware's Trap Pond make great bass structure.

Chapter 18
Vermont beckons

I have honed my kayak fishing skills in Maryland. Those skills have been augmented by guided kayak angling trips in Tampa, Florida. But I wondered what I could I do in a new area without a professional guide. I put that query to the test in the summer of 2016.

My good friend Terry and his wife Allison were spending the summer in Vermont in a quaint lakefront cabin on South Hero Island in Lake Champlain. They invited my wife Linda and I to join them for a week and of course we accepted their generous offer.

In addition to enjoying the scenic Vermont countryside and the Green Mountains and visiting nearby Burlington, Terry and I got out on Lake Champlain three times. He graciously let me use his yellow Hobie Outback while he paddled his Santa Cruz Raptor.

Terry in Lake Champlain. Just like old times in the Chesapeake.

I brought a medium light spinning rod to Vermont and one Plano box of lures that held a sampling of my favorite homemade spinners and jigs and a few paddletails and plugs. Terry augmented that by lending me one of his spinning rods. He showed me a plastic worm popular in the area for smallmouth bass rigged weedless and weightless. I tied that to his rod and used a 1/8 oz. jig and 3 inch paddletail on my rod – essentially the same setup I use when casting for speckled trout in Florida and stripers in Maryland.

Lake Champlain is enormous body of freshwater. It is 125 miles long and has a surface area of 490 square miles. It is bordered with rocky banks and its waters are exceptionally clear. Often I could see the bottom in 10 or more feet of water. When I couldn't see the bottom I could see the tops of subaquatic vegetation sprouting from an unknown depth.

Typical rocky outcropping in Lake Champlain.

As stated earlier in this book, I prefer casting over trolling. So cast I did. I took a passive trolling approach with the weedless worm. I simply let it dangle from the back of my Outback as I maneuvered for casting.

As luck would have it, I caught my first smallmouth with the worm within 10 minutes of launching. In fact, I didn't know I had it. Terry told me I had a fish on the line because he could see my trailing rod bouncing. I was busy tossing a paddletail toward the shoreline and not paying attention to the rod with the weedless worm.

I soon learned that Lake Champlain smallmouth bass were very different from those I had caught during my river wading years in Maryland and Pennsylvania. I had caught hundreds of smallmouth in the upper Potomac and Susquehanna but few were as large as my first Lake Champlain bass.

My fist Lake Champlain smallmouth.

That fish was an omen of good things to come. In fact, they got better. For each of our three outings Terry and I caught fish like the one in the above photo. They were the norm – 13 to 15 inches and great fighters. Most went airborne after they were hooked then they dove for deeper water and bent our rod tips to the water line. They were great fun.

Like I normally do when casting, I worked structure. The rocky shorelines were inviting targets and I hammered them. I tossed my jig and paddletail toward them and picked up a fair number of smallmouth bass. I also loosened the drag on my trailing rod so I could hear striking fish pull the line. That happened frequently and on one occasional I had a fish on both lines at once.

But my best discovery was that the bigger fish were not hovering near shorelines. They were 75 to 100 yards from shore in the plentiful grass beds I could see below my hull in the clear water. This is a pattern I learned on my trips to Tampa. Vegetation often holds fish. There was a casting lane of about 2 to 3 feet between the top of the plant growth and surface of the water. I decided to run one of my 1/8 oz. spinners just over the top of the vegetation. That encouraged the bigger fish to come charging out of the grass toward the pulsating spinner blade. I saw many of them strike the spinner in its return trip to my Hobie. The 13 to 15-inch norm suddenly became 16 and 17-inch fish.

And then it happened. I saw a large bass charge my lure. Terry was nearby and he saw the bend in my rod at the moment of hookup. Then we both saw it jump. I immediately began saying to myself aloud, "Don't screw up, don't screw up." Terry got a kick out of that. After several minutes of aerial displays and deep dives I had the fish close to the boat. I reached for the leader, and Terry shouted, "Don't do that. It'll break free. Play it out some more." So I did. I let fish go for another minute or so to completely tire it out. All the while I was hoping my little white perch spinner would hold tight. It did and I finally had a grasp on the bass.

A memorable smallmouth for me.

You can see in the photo that the smallmouth was indeed pulled from the vegetation. You can also see "coach" Terry in the background. The bass measured a full 19 inches, my personal best for a smallmouth.

With that catch Terry and I stayed on the grass beds. The vegetation was plentiful and so were the bass in those areas. Terry continued to drag his weedless worm over and through the vegetation while I casted my paddletails and spinners over the beds. I caught several more 16 and 17-inch smallmouth and even brought an 18-incher to the kayak, again on a white perch spinner.

Given the prevalence of the grass beds, Terry and I separated in our individual searches for fish by hundreds of yards as we often do in the Chesapeake. I could sometimes see splashes in the distance around his Santa Cruz Raptor as he landed a fish and he told me he saw splashes around my Outback as I landed mine. We were doing well. It was almost like a striper blitz on the Chesapeake.

In due time I saw Terry slowly paddling toward me. I figured something was wrong and headed his way. When we got to within speaking distance (we had no radios on this trip) he told me he dropped his Boga Grip overboard and it slid down his anchor trolley on its tether to the stern where he couldn't reach it. He asked me to retrieve it.

This was not an unusual event or request. Kayakers frequently help each other on the water to untangle fishing line wrapped around a rudder or to retrieve a lure stuck on the bow of their friend's kayak. I've done many of those on-the-water rescues and been the recipient of the same.

I dutifully maneuvered the Outback to the stern of the Santa Cruz Raptor where I saw the handle of the grip hanging on his anchor trolley. Then I saw the real reason for Terry's visit. A beast of a bass was attached to the Boga Grip slowly swimming in place behind the Raptor! Terry – ever the trickster. The first words I uttered were very unflattering to Terry. I called him a name that strongly questioned the marital status of his parents. And then we both had a good laugh as I detached the grip from his anchor trolley and pulled his catch from the water. I measured it on my Hawg Trough at slightly over 20 inches and handed the fish to him for the following photo.

"I dropped my Boga Grip. Can you get it?"

That was the biggest catch of our visit to Lake Champlain and it was also Terry's personal best smallmouth. During our three outings and roughly 12 hours on the water Terry and I landed between 75 and 80 smallmouth bass equally distributed among us. We caught a few dinks for sure but most of our fish were well-fed healthy bass that gave us that great feeling of weariness that comes from catching a lot of sizable fish. And we each caught our personal best smallmouth.

So I left Lake Champlain very satisfied that my kayak fishing skills were transferrable to other areas. I knew how smallmouth bass behaved in the Potomac and Susquehanna from my many fly fishing sessions on those waters. They are savage predators attracted to movement. I strongly suspected that the paddletails and small jig spinners I brought to Vermont would attract them. I was very comfortable with those lures having used them extensively at home. I had confidence in them and I firmly believe that having confidence in my baits helps me to catch fish with them.

Then there was the matter of structure. With no fish finder to show me changes in depth and bottom contours, I relied at first on visible structure. Fish were present along the rocky shoreline but not the larger ones I was seeking. The clear water revealed another kind of structure, subaquatic vegetation. Running my bait over that growth enticed larger bass to chase my lures. That vegetation was the key to my personal best smallmouth and Terry's. Each of those fish exceeded 4 pounds according to smallmouth growth charts.

I learned that fishing is fishing no matter where you go. Skills perfected on local waters will very likely transfer to new waters in faraway places. But a kayak will make that transfer easier. A kayak keeps you closer to the water, closer to the structure and ultimately closer to the fish. You can observe angling subtleties that you cannot observe in a larger boat. A kayak is a great angling classroom and I believe it is the ideal vehicle to improve your fishing skills. You cannot run and gun for miles in a kayak to find fish. You must be resourceful in a relatively small area and learn to find the fish that are inevitably present but just need some extra enticing on your part. The thousands of casts I've launched from a kayak in Maryland's Severn River and on its Eastern Shore ponds and in Tampa, Florida were each a subtle lesson in working a lure that contributed to my success in Lake Champlain. Once more a small plastic boat provided a wonderful outdoor memory for me, this time in the largest body of freshwater I have ever fished. And again the simple joy of kayak angling was revealed to me in Vermont.

Beautiful Lake Champlain.

Chapter 19
Back to the launch

I've taken you on a much abbreviated version of my fishing life. You know the start and you know where I am now. As I come to the end of this story I thought I'd speculate on where I am going with my kayak fishing. One thing is certain. I like it too much to give it up. I will continue as long as I am physically able. That is why I purchased the relatively light Ultimate 12 paddle kayak. I can see myself transitioning to shorter outings than I presently take in my Hobie where traveling double digit nautical miles is common. Also I expect I will fish more protected waters as time goes on. Fortunately, the Severn River is close to my home and it offers me many opportunities for quiet settings. Plus, it can "fish big" when I have that inclination to head to open waters.

Also I hope to introduce my family to the sport. I am grandfather and when my grandchildren are old enough, I will put both of my kayaks on the water at once. And when my children have time I will do the same, much like I did when they were young in our Old Town canoe. But for now, they are consumed with their own family and career obligations just as I was when I was their age – although I must admit that the demands on young parents seem greater now than when I experienced it.

If nothing else, I hope these pages have validated or perhaps gotten you to think about your own feelings concerning kayak fishing. No doubt you already enjoy it or you would not have picked up this book. But I also know that sometimes we take for granted the things we enjoy and we may overlook the nuances of our activities that actually contribute the most to our satisfaction. I've tried to highlight those things here and to emphasize that kayak fishing is more than catching fish.

Surely, the amity I have developed with those I have met in the hobby has greatly enriched my life. I've gotten to know many good people beyond their nicknames on Snaggedline.com or by which kind of kayak they paddle or pedal. I consider them close friends, not just kayak fishing acquaintances. That is priceless.

The hundreds of hours I have spent on the water in a kayak have not produced one minute misspent. I am truly thankful for the sights and sounds of the Chesapeake Bay. I enjoy it all, from nature's many visual gifts onshore and on the water to the chugging hum of working boat motors, their captains hurrying to retrieve their next crab pot. The ponds on the Eastern Shore provide a serene setting for a most relaxing form of fishing. I loft cast after cast near submerged logs enticing largemouth bass to attack my top water offerings in a flash and a splash. Or I stop fishing and watch the bald eagles circle above me. It's hard to determine which pursuit is preferable. In Florida, a completely different flora and fauna awaits as I work lures in mangrove-lined waters for speckled trout and ladyfish while winter blasts my home waters in Maryland. And Vermont gave me an entirely new kayaking angling experience with strikingly beautiful scenery and large agreeable smallmouth bass. No matter where I am fishing in my kayak the setting elicits the same response – pure enjoyment.

I hope my words here have made you recall similar feelings that you have encountered in your kayak. If you don't have a fishing kayak yet, perhaps I have convinced you to buy one. If I have done either of those things, I have accomplished my goal. Then like me, you will head back to the launch after each outing completely, fully and utterly satisfied by the simple joys of this wonderful activity.

Going back to the launch. Tired but happy.

Chapter 20
The Cliff Notes Version

I realize that this is a short book. But this is also the 21st Century and many have come to expect their information in sound bites, Power Point presentations and Tweets. For those of you who like your data brief, here's a synopsis of the preceding pages:

- I've been fishing since I was little boy, bitten early by the fishing bug. I learned to fish with lures relatively late in life but once I did I never returned to bait. I also became a fly fishing addict, routinely traveling far to reach destinations where I could wade shallow rivers.

- My kayak introduced me to a whole new world of tidal fishing close to my lifelong home. It rekindled and revitalized my interest in fishing and allowed me to meet many like-minded people. My kayak and my kayak angling friends have helped me adjust to retirement.

- Catching fish is fun but so is observing nature up close from my kayak. I've seen many interesting things on the water, some expected and some surprising. And each has enhanced my kayak angling experience. I encourage everyone to not let the pursuit of fish make you blind to the exquisite sights that nature offers.

- Kayak fishing allows you to join others on the water but also gives you great independence to pursue the kind of fishing you prefer. You can truly fish alone in a group in a kayak and still enjoy the camaraderie of close friendships.

- A marine radio is an important safety device. But it can also improve your odds of catching fish and it can provide entertainment. Like a famous credit card commercial says, don't leave home (the launch) without it.

- I don't carry a lot of tackle on the water in my kayak. But what I do bring often serves multiple purposes and therefore has made me a more resourceful and a better overall angler.
- Fly fishing is a quite feasible in a kayak. Furthermore, you do not have to stand to fly cast. In fact, there are good reasons why you should never stand in your kayak.
- In addition to tying flies I have recently begun making jigs and jig spinners. I find it extremely satisfying to catch fish on flies and lures I have made and I offer it as a possibility for all kayak anglers to enhance their own fishing experience.
- Fishing kayaks in general are getting larger and heavier. I argue against this trend not only from the practical standpoint of the difficulty in transporting a heavier boat, but because it takes us farther away from the simplicity of the kayak fishing experience. I have countered the trend by purchasing a second kayak that is a basic lightweight paddle-driven boat.
- Trolling is probably the most common way to kayak fish in the Chesapeake. It's extremely effective for catching stripers large in quantity and large in size. It's also my least favorite form of kayak fishing. There are other ways to catch fish in your kayak. Don't neglect them by getting caught up in the trolling numbers game. If you do, you will forego many of the benefits and advantages that kayak fishing can offer. Expand your kayak opportunities. Don't constrict them by trolling all the time.
- Casting takes skill, not only the physical act of shooting line out over the water, but making sure your fly or lure lands where it can be most effective. Your kayak can position you for optimum casting success. Don't overlook the possibilities that casting from kayak holds to catch fish.
- To paddle or pedal – there are justifications for each.
- Skunks happen. Get back on the water as fast you can to improve the aroma of your kayak and your outlook.

- Joining your kayak friends for overnight fishing trips on distant water is great fun. Generally, compatibility reigns among good friends fishing together. But sometimes it doesn't.
- I am fortunate to have excellent local waters to fish. My favorite site is the Severn River. It offers big water and creeks and tidal ponds. The fish species are varied and active most months of the year. Plus, the river is very accessible thanks to an excellent public launch site.
- The Chesapeake Bay Bridge is a nearby portal to superb and varied fishing locations.
- A kayak is a great angling classroom. The lessons you learn in it will transfer easily to distant waters.
- Kayak anglers share a wonderful hobby. The privileged ones appreciate all of its virtues, not just that it allows them to catch a lot of fish.

The author wishing you many enjoyable kayak fishing journeys!
Photo courtesy of John Veil.

A final word of appreciation

For 37 years my wife has watched me to go fishing without reservation. Indeed, there was a time before an insidious neuro/muscular illness intervened in her life and took away her mobility that she would join me on the water. She could throw a fly line with great accuracy, allowing the rod to load perfectly on the back cast. She did not overpower the forward motion like many men do when they are learning to cast a fly line. Her loops were tight and her casts long. She fished with me on the Shenandoah and the Potomac and she understood my elation at tricking a smallmouth to rise because she did the same and got just as excited as me when the fish struck her popper.

But even when declining health prevented her from joining me on the water, she never resented that I continued to fish. She never questioned that UPS packages were arriving with regularity at our address containing fishing tackle and fly tying supplies. She never forbade me to leave for another fishing trip with the guys, nor made me "pay" when I returned with a cold shoulder or complaints about what went wrong at home while I was away. She continues to support and encourage me in my hobby today as I fish frequently in retirement with my friends.

My only regret about kayak fishing is that I did not have to buy his and hers Hobies so she could join me on the water. I know she would have enjoyed kayak fishing as much as I do. It's one of the few good things in life we have not been able to share.

Linda, I thank you, I respect your inner strength, and I love you!

43646183R00058

Made in the USA
Middletown, DE
27 April 2019